BEAUTIFUL ENCOUNTERS

A true account of my son's visit to heaven

Written by

SERENA LYNN KUSTRA

E^{xulon}LITE

BEAUTIFUL ENCOUNTERS
A TRUE ACCOUNT OF MY SON'S VISIT TO HEAVEN
by SERENA LYNN KUSTRA

Printed in the United States of America.

Melissa Doyle, Casting Memories Photography.

ISBN 9781498497077

Unless otherwise indicated, Scripture quotations taken from the King James Version (KJV) – *public domain.*

www.xulonpress.com

My Guardian Angel Date

Footprints in the Sand

One night I dreamed I was walking along
the beach with the Lord.
Many scenes from my life flashed across the sky.
In each scene, I noticed one set of footprints in
the sand.
Sometimes there were two sets of footprints,
Other times there were one set of footprints.
This bothered me because I noticed
That during the low periods of my life,
When I was suffering from
Anguish, sorrow or defeat,
I could see only one set of footprints.
So I said to the Lord,
"You promised me Lord,
That if I followed you
You would walk with me always.
But I have noticed that during
The most trying periods of my life
There have only been one
Set of footprints in the sand.
Why, when I needed you most,
You have not been there for me?"
The Lord replied,
"The times when you have seen only
one set of footprints,
Is when I carried you."

Mary Stevenson

♥ For my sons,
you give me hope and inspiration ♥

4/17/2016

So while putting Jackson to bed tonight, I asked him if he sees angels. He says, "Yes sometimes". I ask him "do you see them at night when you're sleeping?" He says, "No they are all around me." I asked what they look like and he tells me "like the tooth fairy, and their wings are like a butterfly." "Mom, I also see lots of rainbows."

Acknowledgments

First, I would like to thank my Lord and Saviour Jesus Christ for always loving me even when I felt unworthy. To my Heavenly Father for giving me the life that I have, and so many blessings, far too many to count. For my husband Jay, who weathered the storm with me, thanks for holding me up and being my rock. To my beautiful boys who make me laugh, and let me know that the struggle is always worth it. To my mom who shared my burden as only another mother could understand.

To my dearest friend Jane, there is no distance that could ever separate us. Our lives were destined to cross paths, and I cannot imagine my life without you.

To my wonderfully dedicated friends Helen and Joy who encouraged me to share my story with the world. I would like to thank my sister in law 'Auntie Kimmy" who has always been the one we could depend on. To my dear friend Veronica Green who opened my eyes to the

Spirit World and helped me to realize that my loved ones are always near.

To all my family and friends who have been on this journey with us for the last five years, I thank you for your love and support.

I would also like to thank my community services, Smith's Physiotherapy for the generous gift of their time. Thank you to The John McGivney Children's Centre for their wonderful facility and amazing staff, a safe haven we could turn to for support and understanding.

Holland-Bloorview Children's Rehabilitation Hospital, there is no way to thank you. You all individually and unitedly brought my son back to a place of independence. You gave my son his life back. There are no words to express my gratitude; I will never forget any of you.

Dr. David Suzuki Public School, the faculty and our entire community for embracing my son, for taking him under their wings and showing him the love and support that he so desperately needed.

To my earth angel Kathy, I know that God brought us together to complete this project. Our friendship was divinely aligned, and I am privileged to have you in my life.

Lastly, I would like to thank my son for showing me the wonders of Heaven, and letting me truly appreciate this beautiful life we are meant to live; to find joy in the simple things and letting today be just that….

Serena

Heaven; /Definition of Heaven by Merriam-Webster

A place where good people are believed, in some religions to be rewarded with eternal life after death.

John 3:16

For God so loved the world, that he gave his only begotten Son, that whosoever believeth in him should not perish, but have everlasting life.   KJV

Prologue

Heaven always seemed more of a concept to me than a physical place. Growing up in a Roman Catholic home, I wondered if I would make it through purgatory to get a chance to see it. At the age of 25, I became a born again Christian baptized through full immersion at First Baptist Church of Windsor. My Pastor, Reverend Rosetta O'Neil helped me to see Christ in a completely new way. She helped me to see that the Holy Spirit is inside of me, I am now able to carry my best friend with me everywhere I go. All I need to do is call on Him and He is right there.

I no longer go through life worried or stressed out. I no longer feel the need to fill my life with things. I have finally found a joy that is never ending and a peace in my heart that no one or anything can take away. I feel that my greatest responsibility to my children is to teach them to lean on God with everything they have and He will always make a way.

I want my boys to know that no matter what life throws at them God already has it worked out in their favor. I begin each day thankful, thankful to be alive and thankful that I am able to do my best to serve my Heavenly Father. I ask Him to use me, to let His will be done in me that I may spread a bit of heaven right here on earth. If any of you are like me, you must ask yourself "what is my life purpose?" It has taken me forty-three years to come to the realization that I am special and unique in my own right and that perhaps I am doing exactly what I am supposed to be doing with my life. Maybe the simple, ordinary things that I do that may seem of no consequence to me may in fact be a big deal to someone else. I think that by just being our best selves, we are doing all that we need to do.

Looking back, I had been going through life on autopilot. Getting out of life just what I was expecting, nothing more. It was as if my prayers had been falling on deaf ears.

Maybe this is all God has planned for me. To be a wife and mother working a full time job and juggling both like most of society. I had been programmed to think that this was a good life, and maybe it was, but somehow it always felt like something was missing. I always had a sense that there was something greater that I was meant to do.

It was not that I was unhappy, quite the contrary; I felt like I was living the dream. After all, I had two great kids, a solid marriage, nice home, great friends and a good job. What more could you want out of life? Little did I know back then, God's will for my life was about to be revealed to me.

The comfortable secure life I had known would be taken from me only to be replaced by fear, doubt and uncertainty of what the future would hold. God had other plans for me and I had lost all control to stop it. I now realize the control was never mine, God directs each of our footsteps and leads us down our chosen paths. As you read on, you will see God's plan for my life unfold and just what led me to write this story.

CONTENTS

Chapter 1: The Second Born. 19

Chapter 2: The Diagnosis. 23

Chapter 3: The Transport. 27

Chapter 4: The ICU. 31

Chapter 5: The Church on the Hill. 34

Chapter 6: The Wait. 36

Chapter 7: Out of the Woods. 39

Chapter 8: The Reunion 43

Chapter 9: Therapy Begins 46

Chapter 10: The Decision. 49

Chapter 11: The Primary. 51

Chapter 12: The Placement 55

Chapter 13: The Recovery 58

Chapter 14: RMH 60

Chapter 15: The Revelation 64

Chapter 16: Grandpa Eddie 66

Chapter 17: Moving On. 71

Chapter 18: Settling In. 74

Chapter 19: BIRT WING. 77

Chapter 20: The First LOA. 97

Chapter 21: The Stander 101

Chapter 22: Beautiful Encounters 105

Chapter 23: Coffee Anyone? 107

Chapter 24: Friends through Circumstance 109

Chapter 25: Front Page News. 113

Chapter 26: Progress.. 116

Chapter 27: RMH and the Canadian Open. 118

Chapter 28: Recollections.. 121

Chapter 29: Blessings from a Stranger. 123

Chapter 30: Unlikely Friendships.. 126

Chapter 31: Fitting in 128

Chapter 32: Sacrifices of Love 132

Chapter 33: The School at the Top of the Hill.. . . . 134

Chapter 34: The Stairway to Heaven 138

Chapter 35: The Benefit 141

Chapter 36: Transitioning Home 144

Chapter 37: The Entity. 148

Chapter 38: The Spirit in the Room. 151

Chapter 39: The Clearing.. 154

Chapter 40: Voices 157

Chapter 41: Make a Wish.. 159

Chapter 42: Heaven Talk, between Brothers. 161

Chapter 43: The Chamber-HBOT Therapy.. 164

Chapter 44: Worn 168

Chapter 45: The Tall Stranger.. 170

Chapter 46: Cherished Memories 172

Chapter 47: These Days.. 176

Epilogue 189

Chapter One
The Second Born

H e came into the world quickly and perfectly, weighing 7lbs, 7oz; our precious miracle. He truly was. Jackson was our second son conceived through In-Vitro Fertilization. The doctors told us that this was our only hope of having children. After having gone through the emotional highs and lows of IVF, my husband Jay did not want to see me go through this yet again. I always knew that I wanted more than one child and so I pleaded with him to try once more.

After numerous hormone therapy shots, ultrasounds and office visits, it was time to see if we had created a baby. We anxiously awaited the phone call from the doctor's office letting us know if we had a viable embryo to implant. My heart sank as the nurse told me we only had one embryo that survived. The odds are not very high with only one, but they assured us that this embryo looked good.

We head over to the doctor's office for a procedure called "The Transfer". This is where they implant the embryo into my body. My husband and I go home and we wait...A couple of weeks later, back to the doctor we go for an ultrasound. To our amazement, we are pregnant! We thank God for this blessing; our baby beat the odds. Nine months and a perfect pregnancy later, Jackson Edward Kustra is born.

My husband brings big brother Lincoln now age three, up to the hospital to meet his new baby brother. It was love at first sight. He was fascinated at the miniature perfection that Mommy created in her belly.

Once we were home with our new bundle, life fell into a routine, although a very busy one. Jackson was a very happy baby with a ready smile for anyone who looked his way. He hit all the usual milestones–although because he loved to eat, he was always big for his age. He seemed to grow up so fast. Perhaps it was because he was the second born and always trying to do what his big brother did. Life seemed almost perfect, and then at the age of two, the unthinkable happened.

It was a typical day like any other. I was at work as an office manager for Investors Group while my husband was working the day shift at Chrysler. I had asked my mom to watch Jackson since he had not been feeling well the day before. I phoned her in the afternoon to check on how he was feeling and she said he had a good day. He ate lunch, played outside and even went down for a nap. It was when he woke up that she noticed something was wrong.

She was folding a basket of laundry in front of the TV, watching some afternoon talk show, when she heard something. She turned around and found Jackson standing at the top of the stairs. He had gotten out of bed, and instead of coming down like he typically would, he stood there with his arms outstretched, reaching for Grandma.

When she asked him what was wrong, he only whimpered and held out his arms to her. She found it odd that he wasn't speaking since he always talked a mile a minute. She picked him up and brought him downstairs to watch Dora the Explorer, his favourite show at the time. She noticed that he was unusually quiet as he sat gazing at the television. Grandma knew there was something wrong, but she assumed as anyone would, that it was just another childhood ailment.

When my husband got home from work, he came in through the front door, which he typically did. Jackson was still on the couch when he walked in and he said "Jack, Daddy's home". Jackson did not seem to hear or sense him; he never even turned around. Jay had to walk directly in front of him for Jack to realize he was in the room.

I was laying on the table at the chiropractor's office when my cell phone rings. It's Jay, asking me to come home because there is something wrong with Jackson. When I pull into the driveway, my husband is on the front porch with Jackson in his lap, wearing nothing but a diaper. It was unseasonably warm for September. He looked a bit pale and he was sweating, so I took him from his dad and brought him in the house.

Jay told me that Jackson had been vomiting and was very lethargic. I immediately took over as moms do, wiping his forehead with a cold clothe and administering Gravol to settle his stomach. I thought he had the flu.

I held him and rocked him, but nothing seemed to settle his restlessness. He vomited roughly four or five times, but the last time something changed. When I picked him up his whole body went limp and his head rolled back. I felt like he was Pinocchio and I had just let go of his strings…

Chapter Two

The Diagnosis

I screamed for my husband, "There's something really wrong! He can't even hold his head up!" As Jay scrambled to load Jackson in the car, we agreed he would head over to the hospital while I arranged with neighbours to watch Lincoln.

When Jay rushed Jackson into Emergency the triage nurse took one look at him in the stroller and asked how long he had been like this? The nurse then phoned for help and grabbed the stroller right out of his hands. They rushed him through the double doors into one of those ominous rooms where people are given little hope of survival. There was a team of approximately eight doctors and nurses around his bed trying to get vitals and administer an IV. Jackson was crashing fast and they could not locate a viable vein, they had all collapsed.

My husband watched in horror as the doctor produced a cordless drill, much like the one he uses around the house. Not knowing what was happening, Jay watched as they froze his shin and began to drill through the bone in his right leg. He could only watch on in desperation as they tried to save our son. They still could not insert an IV and proceeded to drill into the bone of his left leg without freezing in order to give him life-saving medication. This procedure is known as intraosseous Infusion. It is the process of injecting directly into the marrow of a bone to provide a non-collapsible entry point into the systemic venous system. This allowed the doctors to provide him with fluids and medication because intravenous access was not possible.

I arrived at the hospital roughly 30 minutes later to discover my son was losing this battle. My husband appeared to be in a state of shock after what he just witnessed. I tried to get answers from Jackson's paediatrician who had been called in to assist. As he was reviewing the image of the CT, he showed us the dark, grainy image of something in the lower part of our son's brain.

He suspected that our son had contracted a viral infection of the brain. At this point, I was quite concerned that it was meningitis. He said that if his diagnosis was correct, he had only seen two other cases of it in his entire 25-year career. They wouldn't be able to confirm anything until more tests were run. Jackson was settled into a room on the paediatric floor and we had to wait until the following morning to see what other tests were needed.

Doctors told us the next morning that they would be performing a spinal tap on our two year old. We were sick with worry because I had heard this was a very painful test. They led us into a room where they instructed us to place Jackson face down on the table. I thought I was going to faint, I could not believe what was about to happen. At the very last moment, a nurse came into the room and told us the procedure would not be necessary. I was so relieved I began to cry. The doctors then decided to put Jackson into the MRI right away.

Jay and I held hands outside the door to the MRI Department and with our heads bowed, we prayed like we never prayed before.

After only ten minutes, the Doctor came out looking grim. He said, "Mr. & Mrs. Kustra, your son has a blood clot in the brain". I couldn't believe what I was hearing, how could this be? I remember phoning my Mom in a state of shock and telling her the news. I will never forget the terror in her voice, after all it was my mother who gave me my babies, as she had been the one who paid for our IVF treatments. She had so wanted us to be parents. Due to the cost of my two pregnancies, she calls my boys "Grandma's two nuggets of gold".

I remember hearing the doctors talking about Jackson and his "stroke". At the time, I could not correlate the meaning of blood clot with stroke. Like every parent of a sick child, you wonder why us? Would my perfect baby boy live? If he did, would he be the same? I can tell you that five years later, the answer would be no. Those were fear filled days...

Chapter Three

The Transport

T he next thing we knew, the doctors were on the phone with Children's Hospital in London. I think our small town hospital realized that this was out of their league. They considered flying Jackson by air ambulance, however there was a very bad storm that night. They decided on ground transport instead. Jay and I decided that he would ride in the ambulance and I would go home and pack a few things since we had another child to consider and we didn't know how long we'd be gone.

After arranging for Lincoln and our dog Cisko to stay with neighbours, I grabbed our bags and headed for the highway. I wasn't far behind the ambulance at this point, and I remember praying the whole way there.

I asked God to please spare my son; he was a miracle after all. I asked myself, why would God give us this child only to take him away? I asked the Father for His mercy and grace to let us keep him. Between praying, and crying, my phone ringing the entire way, the two-hour car ride was finally over. We had arrived at Children's Hospital in London. We had no way of knowing this was about to alter the entire course of our lives.

We had contacted all of our family at this point to let them know what was happening and it so happened that my husband's brother, Sam, had been working in the Hamilton area. When he heard that my son was being transferred to London, he made his way back to us. He was roughly two hours from the hospital in London and made it to us in half that time. He was Jackson's Godfather and had a very special relationship with both of my boys.

When we arrived at the hospital, Uncle Sam was there waiting. We all looked at each other and broke down crying. How could we possibly be in this situation? This is something that happens to other people; it was surreal.

A team of neurologists and nurses were awaiting our arrival. They had been briefed on my son's case and had an action plan already laid out. All my husband and I could do now was to step back and let the experts take over. As we watched from the foot of his bed, they began their own assessment of Jackson. My son was pleading for Mommy and Daddy to help him; we could read it in his eyes. He could no longer talk; his speech had been robbed by the stroke.

The doctors decided that Jackson needed another MRI right away. My son began to cry as the nurse wheeled his gurney into the hall towards the MRI dept. I asked if I could lay with him, and so I hopped on the gurney for the ride down. I stroked his hair and told him everything would be all right. I remembered to pack his favourite blanket and soother, the things that brought him the most comfort. Little did we realize that along with his speech, he also lost the sucking sensation, and therefore could no longer use his favorite orange pacifier. The best he could do was roll it around in his mouth before it fell out. It was truly heartbreaking to watch.

As Jay and I anxiously waited, we held hands and prayed once more, asking God for mercy and strength. What we did not realize was just how much worse things had become. After reviewing the imaging with us, the doctors gave us news that no parent wants to hear. The clot had grown considerably larger, filling up most of his brain stem. The first 72 hours are the most critical they said, things could go either way.

My God, how could we be faced with this? Our child was at death's door, we might be going home to a family of three. My faith had been tested before, but nothing at all like this.

As we pleaded with the doctors to save our son, we knew in our hearts that they were doing everything possible for him. The rest was in God's hands.

Chapter 4
The ICU

Jackson was immediately transferred from the paediatric floor to the Intensive Care Unit; this was the
ominous wing of the hospital no child should ever have
to visit. Walking past all of those rooms of severely sick
children left you with a feeling of despair. The one thing
I will never forget was the sound of such intense quiet.
None of the babies or children were talking or even
crying. The only sound you heard was the beeping of
the many machines keeping these children alive.

The orderly wheeled Jackson into a room of his own.
The room was too small for all the lifesaving equipment,
so only one parent was allowed in at a time. The nurses
began to hook my son up to the various machines and
IVs required to assist him. So many tubes protruded
from his little body that we could only lay beside him
on the bed. I wondered if I would ever rock my baby to
sleep again.

Our family all wanted to come to be with us but what was the point? Only one person was allowed in his room at a time and we wanted to keep the risk of infection down for all the patients of this unit. However, Jay and I realized that this could go either way, and our son may not make it, this was our family's chance to see him potentially for the last time. Therefore, they filled the small waiting room, each taking a turn to be buzzed in by the nurse. They were able to see him and offer their words of encouragement and love. As they each came out with red-rimmed eyes, all they could offer us was a hug and a prayer. Whether Jackson heard them, we will never know, but something happened to him during those days in the ICU that have changed him forever.

The nurses took pity on us and broke the rules by allowing both Jay and I in the room at the same time. We would take turns lying on the bed beside our son, praying for him and stroking his hair. Although he couldn't speak, we knew he could understand everything we were saying. Jackson would not regain his speech for nearly three months which proved to be the most difficult thing for us to bear. Not being able to hear the sound of your child's voice, the quiet was deafening…

A few of my husband's friends and co-workers made the trip from Windsor to London to offer us support. They brought Jackson a teddy bear for his bed, and they took up a collection at work of more than $2000 to help us with expenses while we were away. Needless to say, we cried like babies. They told us that everyone felt so badly about our situation and they all wanted to do something to help, so they donated to our cause.

By now, word had spread about Jackson's condition. We had no way of knowing the extent of the prayer chain taking place for him. God's devoted were praying for a miracle. When we arrived at Children's Hospital in London, we immediately phoned our Pastor and asked for prayer. Although she preached in Windsor, she lived in Detroit, so we not only had our local church praying, but several churches in Michigan too. My parents' winter in Florida and my Mom called out for help down there as well.

All of Florida was praying for my son. I later discovered that New York was praying, British Columbia, Alberta and Ontario. I could not believe the powers that were working behind the scenes for my child or what was happening with him at the very same time. We now believe it was during this prayer vigil that my son went to Heaven.

Chapter 5

The Church on the Hill

During these first few days, Jay became sick with a cold. He thought it best to see a doctor so as not to bring anything back to Jackson. He also had to fill out forms so that he could remain off work. At this point, we had no way of knowing how long Jackson would be in hospital. The nursing staff advised him that there was a walk-in clinic across the street from the hospital. While he waited for his turn to be called, he pondered our predicament and fear took over once again.

When the doctor came into the room and asked Jay what was wrong, he broke down crying. The floodgates opened and he could not stop it. He told the doctor everything and at the end of it all, the doctor asked if he could pray for him and our family. He mentioned that along with being a doctor, he was also a deacon at his church. He invited us to come out on Sunday and the congregation would pray for our son. We reluctantly left

Jackson's bedside to seek prayer and strength from a room full of God's devoted. We made our way over to Hillside Baptist Church.

These wonderful people welcomed us with open arms, offering prayer, comfort and even the use of their homes. We had invitations to come and stay "as long as you need", by so many beautiful people, all willing to offer us any kind of solace. Looking back, I realize that this church on the hill was what carried us through during the darkest hours. God was faithful, sending us just what we needed.

Chapter 6
The Wait

The worst part of all was the waiting; hour after hour sitting at his bedside, waiting for some sign of hope. The stroke had robbed our son's ability to walk, talk, eat, or even hold his head up. We were dealing with a two-year-old newborn. Would doctors be able to give us our son back? Would he be the same? What kind of life would he have if he pulled through this? These were all questions that Jay and I asked ourselves every day in addition to what every parent of a sick child asks, why us?

We had now been in London for three days while our five year old was back at home wondering what had happened to his family. As a mother, I was so torn; I had two children that needed me, but I had to leave one behind. I felt like I had abandoned Lincoln. I knew he was scared and did not understand, after all, he was only in Senior Kindergarten. He stayed home with

Uncle Nick and Auntie Di, surrogate grandparents who had been in his life since birth. We decided to try to keep his life as normal as possible during all the chaos somehow hoping he would not be affected. This abandonment if you will, affected him more deeply than we could have imagined.

The school suggested that we get him counselling. He was acting out in class, aggressive behaviour they called it. During those counselling sessions, we were later told, he had revealed that all his worst fears were his new reality. He was angry at being left behind not knowing what was happening with his brother. They said he was sad and crying one minute, angry the next. Jay and I knew that as soon as we were able, we had to come home for him. It would not be possible for another week.

During our time in the hospital, we were fortunate to have the use of the Ronald McDonald House. People truly have no idea the extent of the love and provisions that this home affords families. Having this wonderful place to come back to at the end of a long day was a Godsend. Everything you could imagine was provided for us. This very quickly became our refuge, a place we could run to for comfort, security and friendships. We came to know and care for so many wonderful families, all of them experiencing the same pain and anxiety as we were. All of us looking in the mirror and seeing a very uncertain future...

We would bring Lincoln up to the house over the weekends so he could spend some time with us and most importantly his brother. They had a toy room, a library and the use of the computer, so Lincoln had lots to keep himself amused when not in the hospital. Jay and I would tuck Jackson in early on a Saturday night and take Lincoln to the movies or we would use the family lounge room to watch a movie and make popcorn at the house. We tried our best to make Lincoln feel secure and reassured.

There is something to be said about sharing your grief with others who can relate. All of the parents we were fortunate enough to meet were more than willing to share their story.

We would regroup at the end of a long day and have coffee around the big table until late into the night. This became a longed for time of day for us. We looked forward to sharing the highs and lows of our day with these wonderful people. We cried together, laughed together and most importantly prayed together. We prayed that each of our children would have a happy ending to their story.

Chapter 7

Out of the Woods

By now, Jackson had been in hospital for three long weeks. The first four days were spent in the ICU, these were the longest and most agonizing for us. We were not even sure if we would be bringing our child home. God was merciful, he saw him through those difficult first few days. As the doctors would say, he was out of the woods. Jackson was on a daily regiment of injectable blood thinners. The nurse would come in twice a day to administer the shots in either his leg, arm, or stomach. They were trying to break up the clot in order to regain the necessary blood flow to the brain.

The neurologists had done everything they could at this point, now it was time to begin rehabilitation. After a stroke, the first six months are the most crucial; it is when the body undergoes the most extensive healing. The therapists had begun a daily routine of occupational and physiotherapy.

In order to communicate with us, Jackson would give us a 'thumbs up' if we guessed what he wanted. He would also reach across his body with his left hand and pat the pillow, we later figured out this meant "lay with me".

It was a right sided stroke which meant that he had almost permanent paralysis on that side.

The days were filled with doctors coming in and out of his room with nurses changing IVs and giving injections. He was the bravest two year old I could imagine, he would not even cry when he received these shots. He would in fact watch the nurse and smile as if he knew these injections were making him better.

His meals were given to him through a tube in his nose that fed down into his stomach. This is known as an NG tube, (nasal gastric). These are not meant to be permanent so the doctors had been discussing the need to have a more permanent solution in place. They wanted to give our son a feeding tube directly into the stomach, or a G-tube as it is commonly known. This procedure would require surgery and Jay and I were not yet ready to go down that road. They left us with some literature to read and told us we could decide later. I think the doctors could see this ordeal taking a toll on both of us.

The highlight of our days was that we now had family and friends coming to visit on a regular basis. We looked so forward to the support of everyone back home. The hard part of these visits was the look of sorrow on everyone's face when they saw what had happened to our healthy child. The former Jackson was your typical rambunctious two year old, and now we wondered if he would ever be the same.

Now that he was on the road to recovery, we asked the doctors for a pass to be able to bring Jackson to church on Sunday. The congregation of Hillside Baptist Church had been such a blessing to us, praying for us, and for the healing of our son. We wanted them all to be able to see how their prayers had been answered. That Sunday, Jay and I were so nervous bringing Jack out of the hospital, away from the safety of the nursing staff and yet we were so excited for everyone to finally meet him.

As we entered the church, pushing the stroller, all heads turned to see as we walked up the centre aisle towards the pulpit. As I remember, everyone stood and began clapping and shouting halleluiah for he had truly overcome! Jackson was the miracle everyone had been praying for. Looking back on that time, this church was our refuge and our strength. These wonderful followers of God lifted us up when we had nothing left to give.

Journal Entry:

Monday Sept 19, 2011
Lifted your head off the pillow a few times.

Rolled from your side onto your tummy! Scared me because you were faced down in the pillow, thank goodness I was here.

You had a follow up MRI with sedation so you slept quite a bit. Good news, no change in your MRI.

We hung out in bed together and watched Treehouse

Daddy went home to see Lincoln.

You received flowers and a get-well card from Kelly & Dan

You received a balloon bouquet from Uncle Dave and Aunt Bonnie & Family

Two nurses from PCCU visited to see how you were doing.

Chapter 8

The Reunion

I t was finally time to go home and get Lincoln. He had
not seen his brother since he was so swiftly taken
to the hospital. Both Jay and I were anxious about this
reunion. We were afraid of Lincoln's reaction to his
brother since he had no way of knowing just how bad
things were. We tried sheltering him from the fear and
uncertainty of it all. We had a hard enough time coming
to terms with it ourselves as parents.

In so many ways, he had lost the brother he once
knew; the brother and playmate that he once had.
Gone would be the days of them playing catch, running through the sprinkler, riding their bikes, for that boy
could no longer do any of those things.

At this point, the doctors could not give us a long-
range forecast. They were hopeful because Jackson
was so young and still had so much growing to do. His
brain was very plastic they would say. Plasticity would

be a term we would hear repeatedly over the next few years.

The doctors were also careful not to give us false hope. They said that with the severity of the stroke, it would be most probable that he would have deficits to some degree. Little did we know, five years later, our son would still be walking with a significant limp, and be attending physiotherapy three days a week.

The day finally came when we walked our five year old up to the paediatric unit of Children's Hospital to see his brother. These smells had become all too familiar, the walk from Ronald McDonald house was often the only fresh air we would get all day. How strange that such a foreign and sterile place could feel like home.

As we entered Jackson's room, he lay facing the window. When he heard us, he turned towards the door. He was probably expecting it to be yet another nurse coming to check on him. When he saw his brother, there was instant recognition in his eyes! Jackson broke out into a big lopsided grin and patted his pillow for Lincoln to come join him.

Lincoln immediately hugged his brother and told him how much he missed him. He climbed up into his bed, which had zippered sides to prevent him from falling out, and zipped them both in as though they were in a tent. Lincoln kept asking Jackson questions but he couldn't understand why he wasn't getting any answers. We had to explain to him that the stroke had taken away his ability to speak. He asked us "when will Jack be able to talk again?" To this we had no answer; it had already been three weeks and he had not uttered a word.

When friends and family got word of Jackson's stroke, they all wondered if it would affect his memory. Out of love, our neighbour Doreen put a book together for our son called "JACK'S BOOK". She came over and took pictures of our house, of our dog, Jackson's room, our vehicles, his toys, the pool and just about anything else that would help him remember who he was and what his life was like. He was only two and I thought how much do two year olds remember anyway, let alone now that he has had this traumatic brain injury. Yet, to this very day, he still pulls out his special book and reminisces about what Auntie Do did for him.

Chapter 9

Therapy Begins

Our days were now filled with therapy appointments. We also had daily visits from family and friends. These were the highlights of our day. Jack thoroughly enjoyed these visits; it was as if home were brought to him. Everyone came bearing cards, flowers, toys, books, anything but food, since he still could not swallow on his own.

Therapy consisted of occupational and physio. They were trying to get some movement in the right hand and arm. Occupational therapy was also working on his swallowing. After approximately two months, he could swallow a half teaspoon of applesauce, under direct supervision. If the food went into his lungs he could aspirate, which could lead to a lung infection. This saddened us for this child was born hungry! There was nothing that Jackson loved more than food. We wondered if he even remembered what eating was. Jay and I felt so bad, we would take turns going out into the hallway to eat a bagel or muffin so as not to bring food into his room. We didn't want him to even smell it because we knew he couldn't have anything.

The occupational therapist brought in a special chair for Jackson during feeding times. He could now hold his head up but could easily fall over. He had to be strapped in so he could remain as still as possible. She would begin with a half a teaspoon of applesauce on a spoon to see if Jackson had the ability to swallow it without difficulty. She held a stethoscope to his throat and listened to the sound of his swallowing.

When you think of all the things that we do daily without any thought at all, it is amazing how much we take for granted. We did not realize how much thought your brain puts into simply swallowing. Your brain tells your mouth, tongue, lungs, etc. what to do and when. All of this is involved to help you swallow. We now realized that this was why Jackson could not suck on his soother anymore. He had his favorite one for nap times which we made sure, when we left home, to bring along with his favorite blanket. When we would offer it to him for comfort, he would put it in his mouth, but then would spit it out because he had lost the sucking sensation.

Most parents are looking to trick their toddlers into giving it up or throwing it out, but for us, we wanted our baby back. We would give anything to rock him to sleep with his orange sucky in his mouth. Our sweet baby boy had to grow up way too fast, he lost so much precious time...

Chapter 10

The Decision

W e could no longer put off the decision of surgery. The doctors told us it was now time for Jackson's NG tube to be removed. As afraid as we were, we understood that it had to be done.

The morning of the surgery, as Jackson was wheeled down to the Operating Room, Jay lay beside him on the gurney. I held his hand and walked next to them. We were trying to be brave for his sake. It's as if he knew something major was about to take place. He seemed afraid and would not stop crying. We reassured him that the doctors were finally going to take the tube out of his nose (which he hated) and try to help him.

We said goodbye to him at the door of the operating room and then broke down crying. As was now our custom, every time they had to take him, we held hands and with bowed heads, began to pray.

Approximately an hour later, the Doctor came in to tell us the surgery was over and everything went very well. This was such a relief; our poor son had already gone through so much. As soon as he woke up, we were right there by his side. He saw us and immediately began to cry. We reassured him that everything was going to be all right and that we would soon be heading back up to his room. This had become his safe place.

He slept most of the afternoon and when he woke up, he was happy to see us. We held up a mirror to his face and he uttered his first words "tube all gone"! He smiled, he was so happy! We were crying; those were the first words he had spoken in weeks.

We asked the doctor if we could bring him to Ronald McDonald House (RMH) for a visit so that we could have a bite to eat. This had become our new routine as long as he was well enough. I think Jackson enjoyed these outings, as it was a change of scenery for him. The staff of the house also enjoyed his visits as they could see the progress he was making. Sometimes we would be wheeling him across the street along with the IV pole, but this time he was free of all tubes. We felt like he had reached a huge milestone. The only evidence of the surgery was some white gauze covering his belly.

At this point, Jay and I finally felt like there was light at the end of this dark tunnel. Our son now seemed to be past the scary stuff and we could finally take a breath.

Chapter 11

The Primary

J ackson had been in hospital long enough at this point to warrant a primary nurse. What this means is that one or more nurses would be his exclusively if they were on duty. We had our favourites and were sure to request them. On this particular night, Nurse Lisa was on duty. She was definitely Jack's favorite!

Lisa had a special way with the kids. She always had on a very bright uniform with some kind of toy hanging from her stethoscope. Always smiling, she was everything a nurse ought to be. She seemed to take a special interest in Lincoln as well. I think my oldest son reminded her of her three boys at home. She had a set of twins who were the same age as Lincoln and so really seemed to know just how to connect with him.

One particular morning a few days before Halloween, Jay and I came up to Jackson's room to find it completely decorated for the occasion. Jackson also had on his new Halloween shirt, he had been bathed, hair combed and ready for the day. We always felt that Lisa cared for our son the way any mother would care for her own children.

We also had Nurse Stephanie, always smiling, forever cheerful. She was a relatively young nurse, but had such deep compassion, everything a caregiver should be. Jackson always lit up when Stephanie walked in the room. She seemed able to get Jack to do almost anything she asked.

Barb was another of Jackson's primary nurses. She took on more of a maternal role for me. She always seemed to know when Jay and I were having a bad day and always did something special to cheer us up. One of my fondest memories was of her having worked a twelve-hour day and yet still finding time to go home and bake cookies for us. She came in the next morning with a couple dozen freshly baked cookies so that we would have something to sustain us through those long hours when we seemed only to survive on coffee. I thanked God repeatedly that we had these strong, loving individuals by our side night and day. They kept us informed, nurtured, and supported through the most difficult of days.

October 13, 2011 @ 2100hrs

Jackson in jam jams for bed. Cried a little x5 min injection given, Jackson back to sleep! Settled with no problems. Brought in a pumpkin for Jackson from your nurses Stephanie & Lisa.
LC

Oct 14, 2011 @ 2400-0700

Jackson you woke up at 4:00am "little man" woke up happy & smiling, took your IV out of foot, you are so "brave", you didn't even cry. You were in such a good mood & laughing, you decided to stay up & watch Tree House until 5:00am. You are to (young to party) HA HA! Party over at 5:30 you went back to sleep. Sleeping well. No morphine given since midnight, only Tylenol.
See you Monday night
Nurse Lisa

Jay and I were emotionally exhausted after a day of surgery and worry. Lisa could see it was taking a toll on us and she offered to sit in our son's room overnight so she could observe him. She said the nights were quiet and that she could do her charting at his bedside.
When we had brought Jackson back from the house, I asked the nurse how I should lift him out of the stroller.

She said to place an arm around his shoulders and the other arm under his knees so as not to disturb the stomach area. As soon as I lifted him, I walked exactly three steps and placed him on his bed and I heard Jackson expel air, I thought he farted.

I could not believe what I saw, it looked like his insides were coming out! My husband and I watched in horror as my son's tube had come out and his stomach contents were emptying on the bed. Thankfully, the nurse was in the room and witnessed what had just happened. She ran out of the room to get help. Seconds later another nurse rushed in and began reinserting my son's g-tube. I will never forget this scene as long as I live.

Just when we thought this nightmare was almost over, it seemed as though fate was having its way with Jackson. How many times did I wish I could trade places with my baby, he had been through more than most would endure in a lifetime...

Chapter 12

The Placement

T he radiologist was immediately called and Jackson was taken for an x-ray to check for placement. Apparently, this is not as uncommon as you might think. A g-tube is held in place by a balloon inside the stomach. Your skin then grows around it to keep it in place. The technician wanted to be sure that it was reinserted properly before anything was administered through it. When this was confirmed, Jackson was given a dose of Tylenol to make him comfortable and Nurse Lisa insisted we go back to the house and get some rest. She would be right at his side and assured us she would call if there were a problem.

We were extremely relieved because we were so tired and just wanted to go back to the house and rest awhile. Once there, our friends informed us that we were invited to Yvonne's house for a get together. She was a wonderful woman who volunteered at RMH. As tired as we were, everyone convinced us that a few hours out might help us feel a bit more normal. For anyone who has ever had a sick child, you can understand how hard it is to be away from the bedside.

Off we went to Yvonne's along with two other families we had befriended. We sat around, talked, laughed, and had a great evening. It was the first time in weeks that we all felt hopeful that there would be brighter days ahead.

We stayed out much later than we anticipated and did not get to bed until after one o'clock in the morning. The sound of the phone woke us. As I looked over at the clock, I realized it was almost five in the morning. The hospital has a direct line to any parent staying at the house.

We were surprised by the call because in all the weeks we had been there, we had never had the phone ring. "Something is wrong with Jackson" I heard the Doctor say, he has spiked a high fever, you need to come over quickly. Jay and I still half asleep threw on our clothes and ran over to the hospital.

When we entered our son's room, there were nurses and doctors everywhere around his bed. What was going on? We were panicked at this point. The doctor had informed us that Jackson was fed some pedialite through his new tube sometime in the night. What they did not realize was that his tube was in fact not in the correct position after all and that all the liquids he had been given were floating in his abdominal cavity rather than his stomach.

This had caused an infection, which resulted in the high fever. The doctor told us she had to get him back into surgery right away to clean out the infection. At this point, I broke down; how much more can my poor child endure? This wonderful doctor sat next to me on the bed and put her arms around me. "As a mother myself, I know how scared you must be. Please know I will do everything I can to make sure your son comes through this ok." I will never forget her kindness, and true to her word, she brought him through. As I lay in Jackson's room waiting, I prayed that God would guide her skilled hands and He did♥

We were called down to the recovery room where we were allowed to sit with our son. When we saw his little body in that big bed surrounded by all those machines, we felt like we were right back to square one. Would this nightmare ever end?

Chapter 13

The Recovery

So there we were again, sitting at our son's bedside waiting and looking on while trying to be hopeful, but let me tell you, I was angry with God. I felt like HE was angry with us and was taking it out on our son. When you are hurting, you are looking for someone or something to blame. I even said to my husband, "God is punishing us, He gave us these two miracles and we are always too busy for them. We work too much, we don't spend enough family time, and we don't play with them enough" I had myself convinced that God was sitting us down and teaching us a lesson. It took nearly three years for me to fully see God's plan revealed to us.

We as a family would not realize the extent of this journey God had taken us on, it all unfolded slowly and deliberately. You see, approximately seven months after the stroke, Jackson at age two and a half, would tell me that he had been to Heaven and sat with Jesus. This was only one account of many to follow over the next few years.

As he lay in his bed, unable to talk, Jay and I looked on feeling defeated. This time post-op, Jackson had tubes coming out of every inch of his little body. We could not even hope to pick him up. We asked the doctor how long he would be like this. We were prisoners to the room again. After having a bit of freedom to be able to take him out in the stroller, or over to RMH, this felt like a jail sentence to all of us. This hospital was beginning to feel more familiar to us than home.

They said the risk of infection was still very high and he needed to be closely monitored. Little did we anticipate Jackson would be flat out on his back in this state for nearly ten days. As a result, he developed pneumonia in his left lung.

The doctors feared this may get much worse, and discussed the possibility of running a central line. We had no idea what this was and once they explained it to us, we were more fearful than ever. This procedure inserts a catheter in through the arm directly into the heart. This is a quick access point for medications and also blood extraction. We were forced once again into the decision of allowing our two year old to undergo another surgery.

Chapter 14
Ronald McDonald House

R onald McDonald House was more than just a place to sleep, it had become our refuge. When nobody else understood, everyone at the house did. We would seek comfort and strength from the other parents living there. After all, no one could truly understand what we were going through, unless they had walked in our shoes.

When I say this house offered everything, I mean that as an understatement. Not only do they offer families shelter, but three meals a day, cooked by wonderfully generous volunteers. These people filled the house with their love, offered their time, and provided all the ingredients necessary to prepare a meal for all of us families. At the end of a long day at the bedside, we looked forward to coming "home" for a hot, home cooked meal.

RMH also offered free long distance so you could keep in touch with everyone back home, free internet, laundry facilities, games room, a theater room, and just about anything else you could think of. When we would bring Lincoln up for the weekend, he had so much fun, he didn't want to go back home.

As we sat around the big table that night, with our newly adoptive family, we asked for advice on this latest surgery. Jay and I were so afraid to have Jackson undergo another procedure. We really did not know how much more our son could endure.

Most of the parents at the house during our time there had premature babies in the NICU. Most, if not all of these children had central lines. The parents reassured us that the surgery was quite safe and routine. This set our minds at ease, and the very next morning, we told the doctors that we would consent to the surgery.

Over dinner that night, our Ronald McDonald family prayed with us for a successful outcome for Jackson. As doctors wheeled our son away from us once again and through the double doors of the operating room, we bowed our heads, held hands and prayed. "Heavenly Father, please guide the hands of the doctors, give them the skill they need to assist our son. We ask for your mercy God please be in the midst of this situation right now, and we ask for healing, in your name, Amen".

Merciful as always, God brought him through. This time, his IV pole would hold Jackson hostage for nearly ten more days. We had never seen so many bags hooked up to an IV pole in our lives. When we asked the nurse what they were all for, she told us, fats were in one bag, nutrients and food in another, antibiotics in another... All Jay and I thought were "great, now we're stuck to the room again."

We had both become so depressed by our son's situation that the hospital had us sit down with a counsellor. We had regular meetings both individually and as a couple. While they counselled us, they told us that statistically most couples do not make it through something like this. "It's like a death, or a divorce, only worse," said the therapist. We realized just how accurate those words proved to be. The only thing that kept us going was our faith and our wonderful family and friends who came up to offer their support.

Chapter 15
The Revelation

Sept 21, 2014

Lincoln was asking Jackson about Heaven and he asked him "What is Heaven like"? To which Jack answered "like a colorful angel house". He then asked him if God likes kids and he said "yes". "Can God grant wishes"? Lincoln asked, and Jackson said "yes".

This is just one of the many conversations that would take place in our home over the next few years. We had come to realize that something wonderfully amazing had happened to our son. We knew that a miracle had taken place with his healing, but we did not know that he would have an intimate relationship with Heaven.

What do parents do with this information? We were shocked and excited, for I think any believer wishes to have an encounter of this kind. When something like this happens to a child, I am not sure they truly understand it. There are times that I have encouraged him to reveal more to me and he would begin to cry. When I asked him why he was crying, he would say, "Mommy, I don't want to go back to heaven". When I asked why, he said, "Because there are no mommy's in heaven". At this point, I would hold him close and reassure him that I was not ever going to leave him.

I realized that God had very special plans for my son and our entire family. After reading many stories of near death experiences, I have come to realize that before we are even born, our soul choses it's destiny. Unbeknown to my son, he selected this for his life's journey.

"Rejoice, and be exceeding glad: for great [is] your reward in heaven: for so persecuted they the prophets which were before you." Matthew 5:12 KJV

Chapter 16
Grandpa Eddie

The first time Jackson revealed anything to me was at bedtime. He was two and a half years old. He told me that he had met Grandpa Eddie. I could hardly believe what I was hearing because my father had been gone for over twenty years. When I asked him where he saw Grandpa Eddie, he told me "in Heaven". The conversation for him was very factual. I was in complete shock and awe! I wanted to hear more, but was a little afraid to push too hard. I wanted and needed more detail, I wanted to know more about my Dad. When I told my husband about this conversation, at first I do not think he believed me. He asked how that was possible when the doctors never once told us that he had flat lined. How could I answer this? I knew it to be true; there was no way a child of this age could make this up.

I would later learn through the help of a spiritual medium, that Jackson had indeed met my father. She told me that she followed my son up a flight of stairs. She then asked me if my house had a set of stairs with a window at the top. I told her no, in order to see the window you had to be in any of the bedrooms. She insisted that the stairs she was seeing were long with a landing at the top and a small window. I was covered in chill bumps as the realization set in. I suddenly knew that she was referring to the house I grew up in. We had a full flight of stairs with a small landing in which my Dad had installed a small octagon shaped window for added light.

She then followed my son into the first room on the right at the top of the stairs. This is where he met his Grandpa. My Dad said he had to go back, it was not his time and that I would be devastated, he needed to return to us. I began to cry, for this was my parent's bedroom that she was describing. It was also the room where my father breathed his last breath.

It was a night like any other, my Dad was working afternoons at the GM trim plant. My brother, then a teenager, was in his room on the phone with a girl. My Mom and I were in the kitchen, she was ironing while I was packing lunches. My father walked through the door at approximately 9:30pm. We were both surprised and asked him why he was home so early. A typical night on afternoons would have brought him in around midnight. He said they let the plant go home early.

My Dad seemed tired, more so than usual, but he asked me "Reenie, would you please fix me a sandwich?" So I did, cheese and lettuce on white with a glass of milk. He sat and watched some TV and then by 11:00pm, we all went to bed.

As was typical for me, I fell asleep as soon as my head hit the pillow. Something woke me up, a sound, was it a scream? It turned out to be my Mom screaming something I could not quite understand. I threw my bedroom door open only to find my Mom on top of my Dad, beating on his chest and screaming for my brother to call 911.

It was as if I was living out a bad dream. My mind was in shock at the scene before me, however my body moved of its own volition. I ran into my parent's bedroom and tried to help my Mom save my Dad's life.

My brother Carl had moved his personal phone call with his girlfriend from his bedroom to the quiet of the kitchen once we all had gone up to bed. Therefore, as the 911 operator was directing him, he was yelling the orders upstairs to us. My Dad began turning blue before our eyes. My Mom yelled down to Carl, "he's turning blue", and my brother yelled back up for us to roll him on his side. My Mom and I did as we were instructed but he seemed to be getting worse and he was unresponsive.

My Mom and I rolled my Dad back over and we tried doing CPR on him. Nothing seemed to be helping and I remember screaming, "Where is the ambulance? What's taking so long?" I knew in that moment, I was losing my Dad. I remember looking into his blank eyes, and pleading with him not to leave me, I cried out to him repeatedly "Dad, I love you, please don't leave me, please don't leave us, we need you." He was only 48 years old.

For anyone who has ever seen it, you will never forget the death stare. I was looking death in the face, even before the paramedics arrived. Even before hearing the doctor's words, confirming our worst fears. It changes you forever.

Even though my father knew The Lord, and I knew he was going to a better place, I was not okay with it. I was angry that God could take away my rock, my security and my provider. How was I supposed to get through to adulthood without my Dad there to guide me?

I was only seventeen. My dad missed so much of my life. I always wondered if he would have been happy with the choices I made in life. I also wondered if he would have been proud of me. I have always told my children about their grandpa, and somehow I feel that they do know him. Ironically enough, Jackson looks a lot like my father. My Dad had a very special quality about him that drew people to him. Jackson has that also. We named him Jackson Edward after my Dad, his nickname is Eddie, as was my father's.

I have come to realize that my father has not missed a single event in my life, he has been watching from Heaven. I do believe he has watched over my boys since the day we brought them home. The very first time we placed Lincoln in his crib, the lights in his room became very bright and then would slowly dim, and this happened every time the baby was in his room. Jay and I would draw comfort from this; we always felt that our fathers, both deceased, were watching over our children from Heaven.

We all come into the world with our own guardian angel, and then as our loved ones pass on, I believe they also become our guardians. One thing I know for sure is that Grandpa Eddie is Jackson's angel, walking side by side with him, offering him encouragement and strength. I draw enormous comfort knowing that my Dad is still very much present in my life.

Chapter 17

Moving On

The doctors were discussing Jackson's discharge from Children's Hospital. It was time for him to move on to a rehab hospital in Toronto, the very best in the country. How fortunate that we had this wonderful resource only four hours from home. They had done all they could for him at this point, he needed extensive rehabilitation. The day was fast approaching for us to say goodbye to the nursing staff as well as our RHM family. Although this was a step forward, we were scared; we were leaving behind the security of everything familiar. Not to mention we were now going to be four hours from home instead of two. This would mean our visits from family and friends would dwindle, leaving us isolated.

It had now been eleven weeks since this nightmare began, and we had no way of knowing that we would be away from home for another four months before it was all over.

My best friend Cisko, my dog, had also been displaced by this illness. Fortunately for us, we have amazing friends who kept our dog the entire time we were away. When Jay and I would alternate coming home, my poor dog was so confused, he didn't know what was going on. Dogs are highly intuitive though and he could sense the heaviness on my heart. What I wouldn't give for this to all be a terrible nightmare that I would wake from. How I longed to take my dog for a walk in the park, like old times...

Jay and I were torn with what to do with Lincoln. We didn't know how long we would be gone and up until now, we had tried to keep his life as routine and stable as possible. After much consideration, we decided we had to go as a family. We pulled him from school in Windsor, and enrolled him in the Toronto District School Board. This would prove to be the best decision for our entire family.

Moving day was upon us and it was time to say goodbye. With tears in our eyes, we said goodbye to all the nurses and doctors who had become our friends. We promised to keep in touch and promised to send photos and updates on Jackson's progress. If you think the hospital was hard, saying goodbye to the Ronald McDonald families and staff was devastating for us.

These people had become our rock; we depended on them for emotional support. I truly did not know how I was going to manage without that support system. Life would prove to be very different at Holland-Bloorview Children's Rehabilitation Hospital.

Chapter 18
Settling In

I rode in the patient transport vehicle with Jackson while Jay and Lincoln followed in the van. We pulled into this foreign place not knowing what to expect. The building was huge and there were beautiful stained glass windows in every color. Could it be possible that this place was really a hospital? We had no idea how capable the therapists were; they would give Jackson his life back. Small wonder they say this was the best in Canada, we lived it, and we can say it is so.

As the nurses unloaded Jackson from the ambulance, we proceeded through double doors where a lovely young woman in a wheelchair greeted us. All around us were people with varying degrees of physical or mental disabilities. Although we had just come from the hospital and were accustomed to seeing sick children, what we saw in this place was quite different. For the first time, Jay and I realized that we now had a child with a disability. Yet the experience opened us up to receiving more blessings then we could ever imagine.

This hospital was vastly different from the one we had just left. They cater to the most severe disabilities. Everyone was so welcoming, and all the patients no matter how disabled all felt the love of this place. Holland-Bloorview gives people hope and lets us see people beyond their disabilities.

After going through the registration process, we took a special elevator up to the family accommodations wing of the hospital. We stepped off the elevator and given a tour of the floor. There was a communal kitchen, although no meals would be provided for us. This would be very different from how things were at Ronald McDonald House. There was also a laundry room on the floor for our convenience.

Finally, we were shown to our suite at the end of the hall. There were only a few of these larger rooms reserved for families who would be staying a while. It was a basic room with a washroom and separate bedroom. Although small, the large windows overlooking the grounds made it seem bright and airy.

This place felt so alien to us after the warmth and comforts of the RMH. We realized that we were truly going through this last phase on our own. We would not have any regular visitors over the course of the next four months. It was just the four of us now and we had to learn how to depend on each other for support. And so we settled in, prepared to make this home for as long as we had to and we were grateful to God for bringing us this far.

Chapter 19

Birt wing

It was now time to see Jackson's room in the opposite end of the hospital. He would be staying in the BIRT unit (Brain Injury Rehab Unit). This is where any child up to the age of eighteen goes if he/she has sustained any type of brain trauma.

The nursing station on this floor was huge. Many children were gathered around it coloring, doing puzzles or playing card games. Some of the children were just lined up and watching the big television. There had to be a couple dozen movies on this rolling cart and the nurse would insert one and line the wheelchairs up in front of it. This seemed like a good idea as the children were always together for company. In the following months, we would often come down in the morning and find Jackson in front of the TV watching movies alongside the other children.

The nurses quickly fell in love with our son and would often request to have him put on their schedule. Our most memorable nurse was Betty who had that special touch with him; he just loved her.

In truth, Jackson was such an easygoing child, who had affection for all his workers. He only had one male nurse the entire time he was there and his name was Randy. Randy would grab Jackson's chubby cheeks and say, "whose cheeks are these? Are these Randy's cheeks?" Jackson would say "NO" with a huge smile.

Rather quickly upon our arrival to the BIRT wing, the Head of Pediatrics came down to assess Jackson. They had previously received all of Jackson's medical records and were very much prepared with an action plan. One of the very first things they did was assess his swallowing.

At this point, because of the disaster with the G-Tube, Jackson was back with the NG in his nose. They quickly determined that he could be placed on a soft diet. The nutrionist ordered him a hamburger and French fries! Jay and I were stunned into silence. The only thing Jack had had up until then besides formula was a bit of applesauce. He had been on a pureed diet when we left London so he had just been upgraded!

Not surprisingly, when the nurse brought in the food tray, Jackson's whole face lit up. He had not seen real food in months. Although he was carefully monitored during his eating, he was able to safely eat very small pieces of food successfully. It would however still be a while before the NG tube could be removed from his nose.

Therefore, the entire team from the physiotherapist, to the occupational therapist, and the speech pathologist would develop a plan that would restore our son to his former healthy state, or so we hoped.

The hard work was about to begin for Jackson, and we had no idea how grueling it would prove to be.

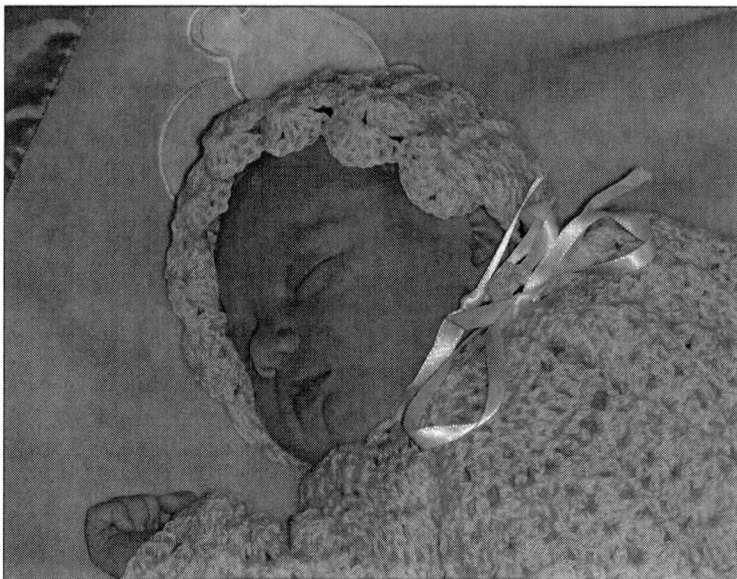

Jackson Edward Kustra, 7lbs 7oz

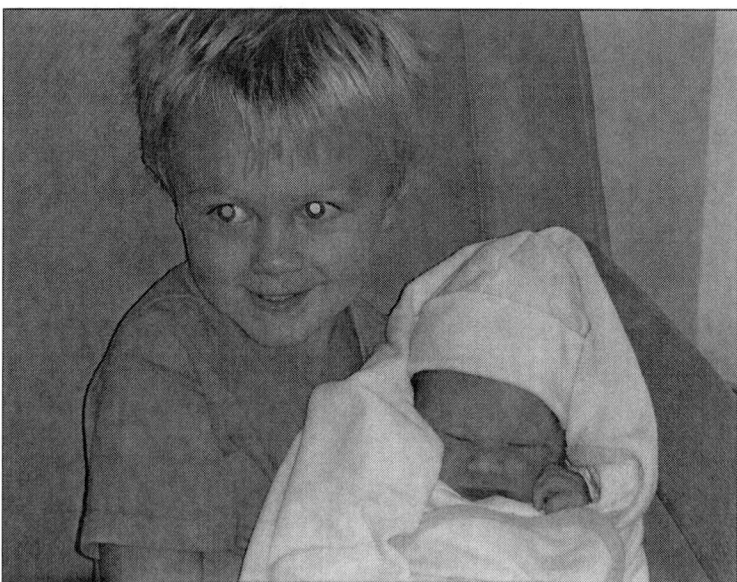

Lincoln & Jackson, I'm a big brother

Jackson, 5 monts old

My baby brother

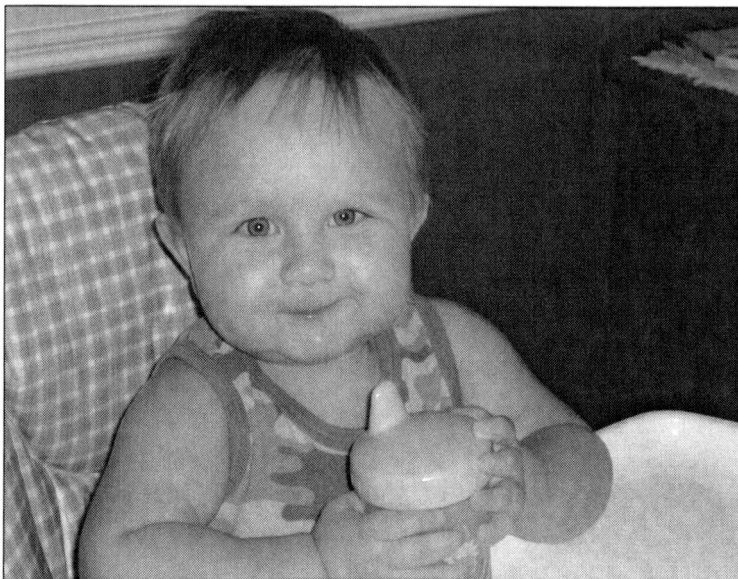

Jackson 1 year old

Best buds

3 months before my stroke

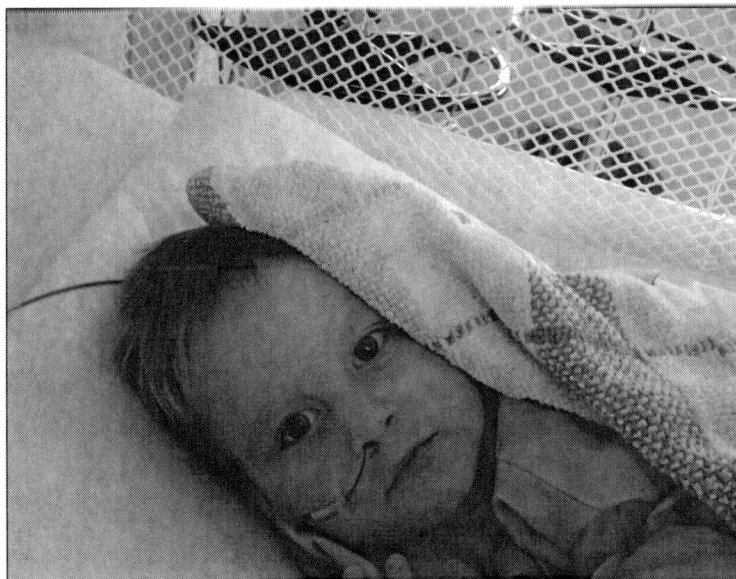

1 month post stroke

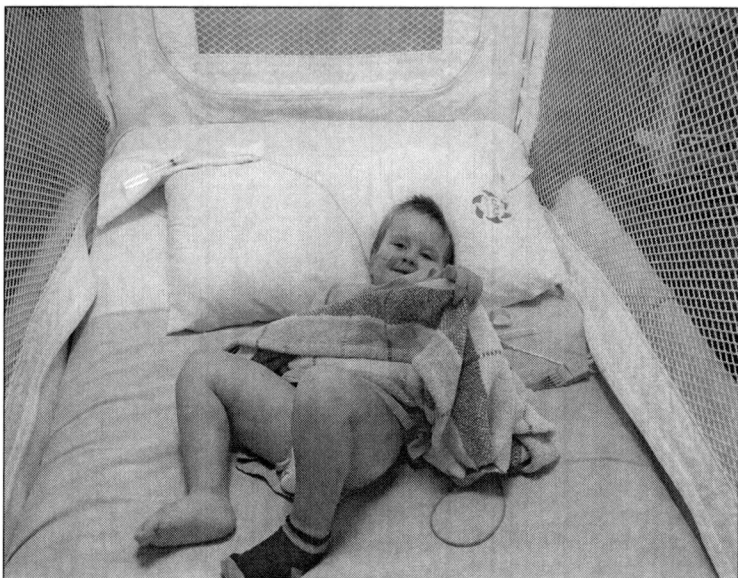

Happy in my bed

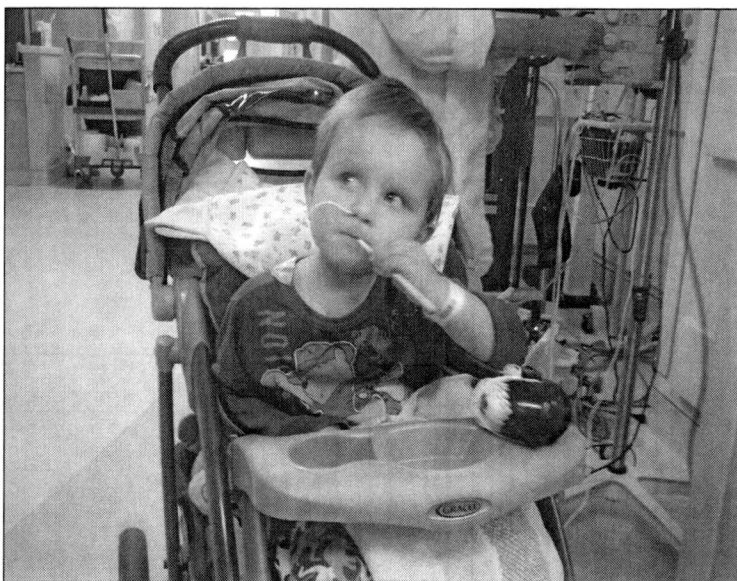

Buggy Ride

Holland Bloorview Kids Rehab Hospital

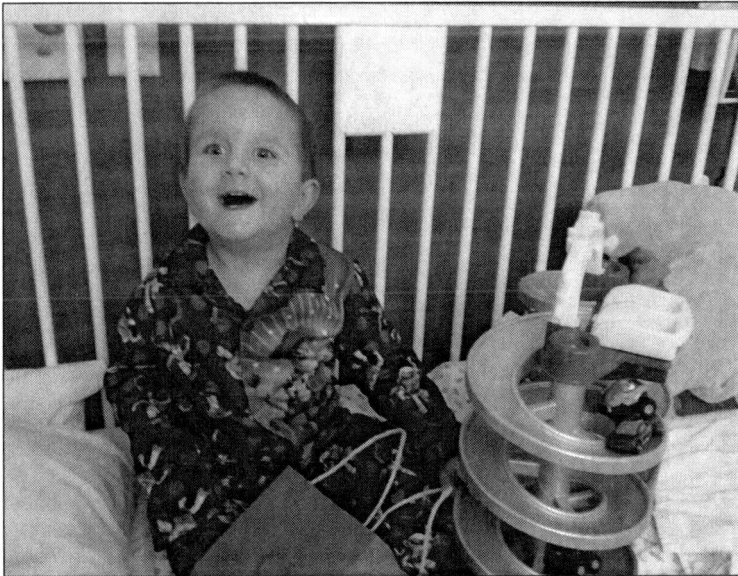

I love my cars!

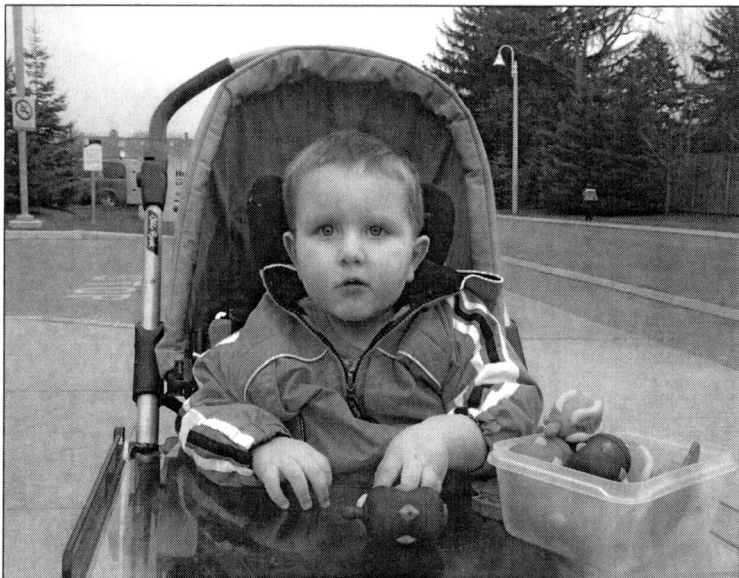

Doing my OT with my toys

Jack in the stander

Waking up happy

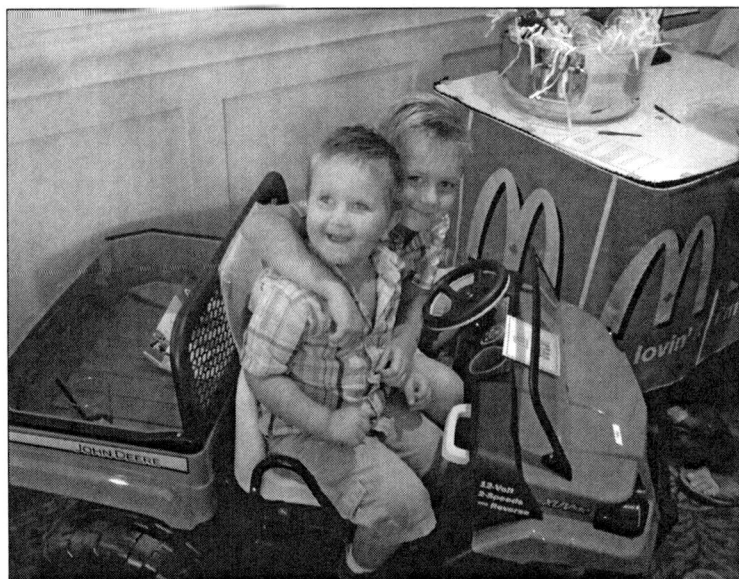

RMH Golf Classic, guests of honor

Boys getting to meet Ronald

LOA for Christmas

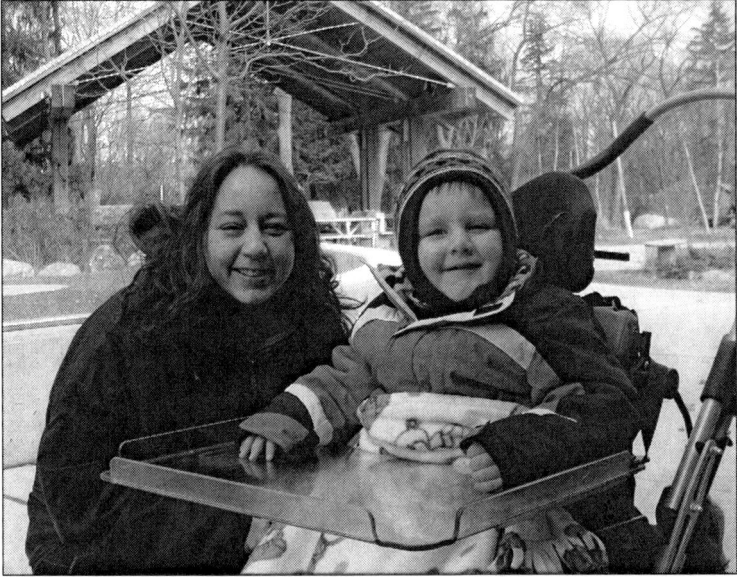

Jack & Auntie Kimmy getting some fresh air

Hanging with Jackson

Auntie Joy came to visit

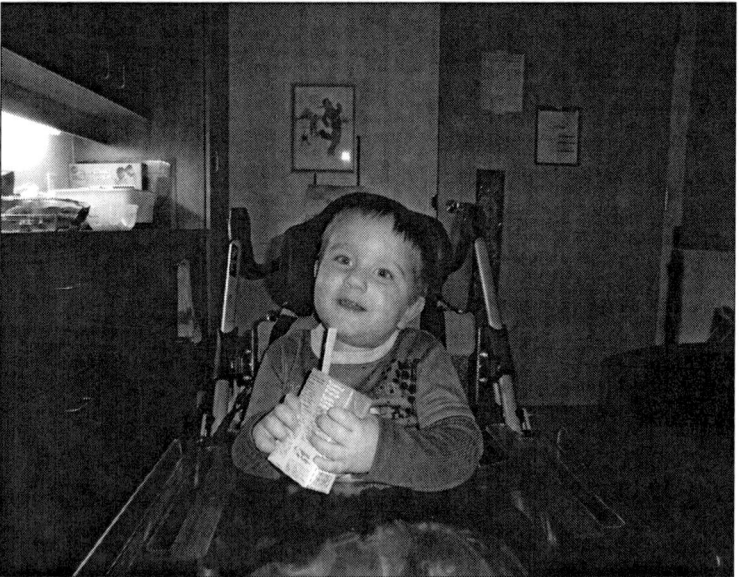

Thickened juice, yummy!

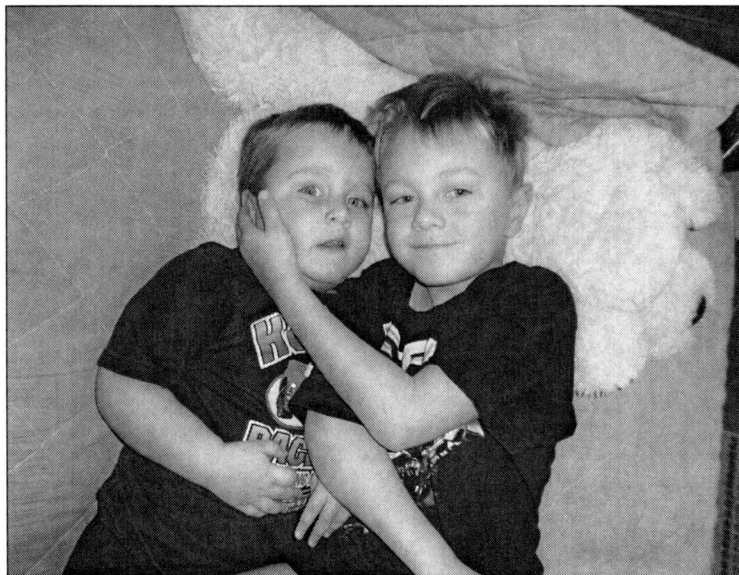
Linc & Jack hanging in our suite

Jackson & Brock

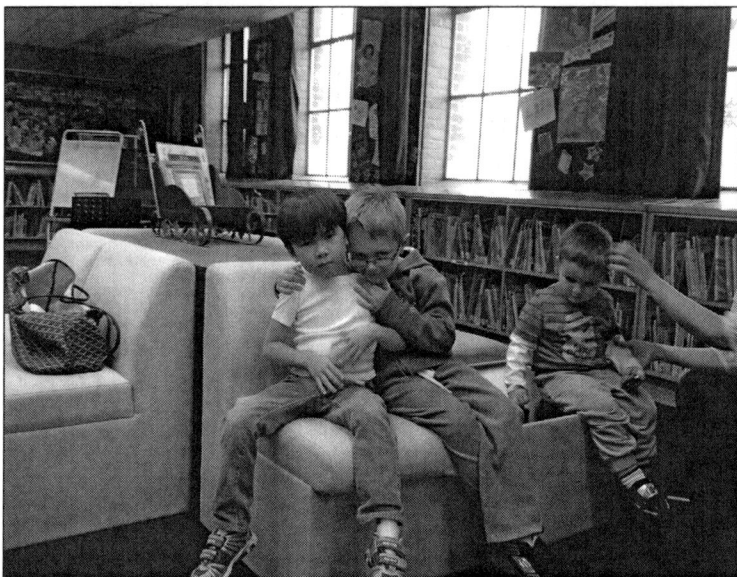

Lincoln and Oliver, the new kids on the block

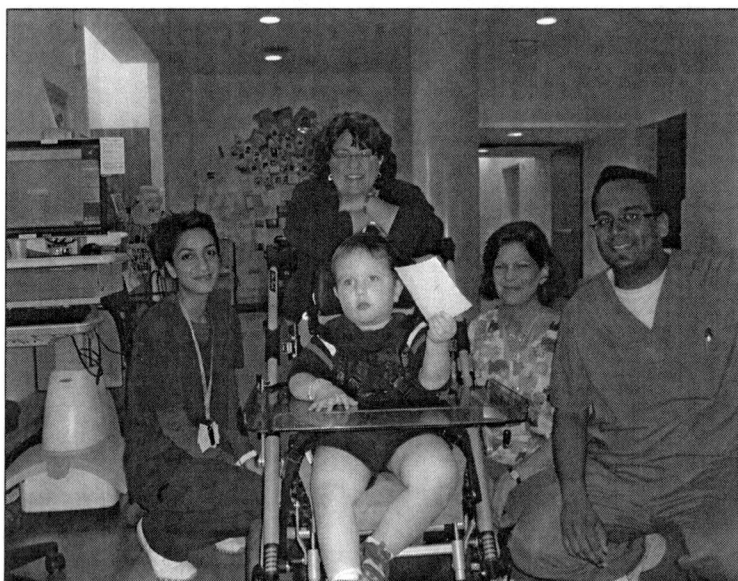

BIRT wing nursing staff

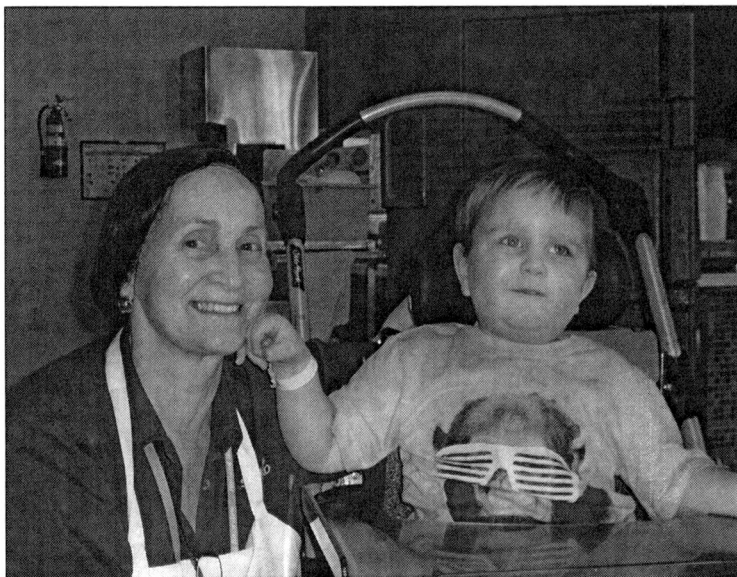

Ms Emma makes my meals

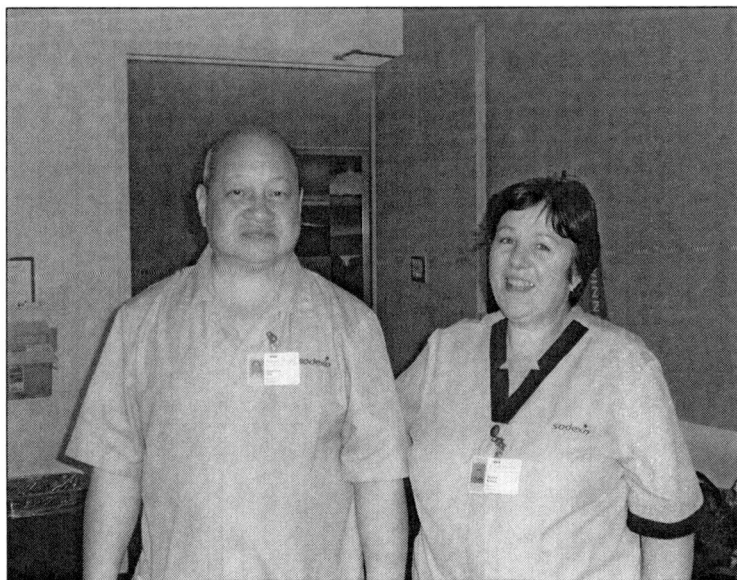

Jose and Berta (house keeping)

Gail (PT), Jackson, and Janet (OT)

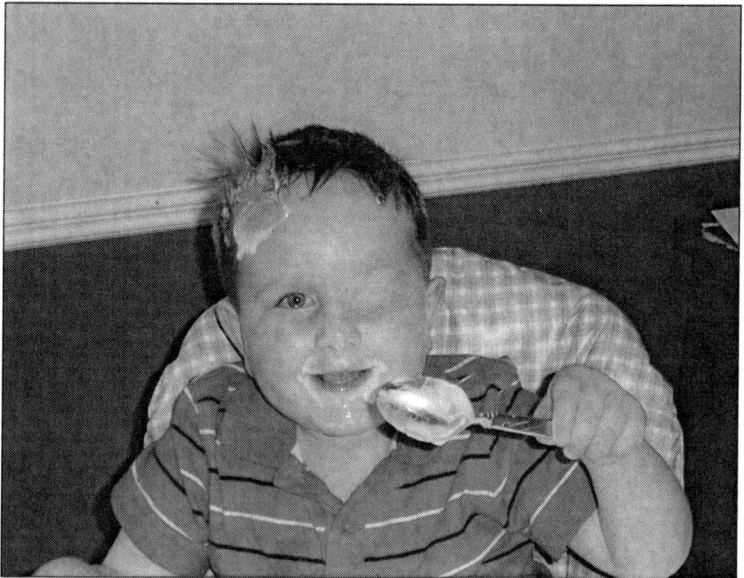

Jackson during eye patching session

Billy Jo and Brock

Going home, it's been 6 months

Welcome home Jackson!

Chapter 20

The First LOA

We had only been at Holland-Bloorview for a couple of days when they announced that we could go home for the weekend. They called this an LOA or Leave of Absence. Jay and I were floored by this news since we had just got there. We had spent a solid eleven weeks in London hospital and had just been transferred here to Toronto, so how is it possible that they could be releasing us for the weekend?

When we shared this news with the boys, I don't think they could believe it either. Jackson lit up like the fourth of July! He had not seen his house, his dog, or any of his friends in nearly 3 months. The Doctors all felt that we had been gone from home for too long and that a small dose of 'normal' might do us all some good.

Before we left, the nurses went through all the necessary steps for providing Jackson's care. He still had his NG tube and so they taught us how to run his feeds and how to check the nasal tube for placement. This entailed placing a stethoscope on Jackson's belly, inserting a syringe of air into his feeding tube and listening for the pop sound that indicates the tube is in place. As long as this was correct, we could proceed to run his feed.

With the hospital supplies packed, including his IV pole, feeding pump and formula, we loaded up the van and both nervously and anxiously headed for the highway. It would feel so good to be home if only for a few days. All I kept thinking about was how much I missed my dog.

That first night home, I don't think Jay nor I got much sleep. We could hear the pump running and the beeping of the machines; it sounded like a hospital room. I will admit I was very nervous without the nurses around. I had come to rely on their presence to give me strength and confidence.

That night when we got home, the first thing I did was walk over to Nick and Diane's house to get my dog. As I was walking up their driveway, I saw Cisko lying in the front window. He saw me coming, jumped up, and ran to the door. He came to me with tail wagging and I starting bawling; I had missed him so much. When we got home, he seemed a bit timid around Jackson he seemed to know that something had happened to him.

As I said, Dogs are very intuitive and he could sense something had changed.

The next day, Saturday, turned out to be quite eventful. The neighbours noticed that our van was in the driveway and so one by one, they all stopped by to see what was going on. They also could not believe we were back home, they all suspected Jackson had been discharged. No, we told them, we were simply home for the weekend. They all said how good it was to see Jackson doing so well and how good it was to have us back again.

Jackson and Lincoln had rediscovered their toys and kept busy playing. Somehow, during this time, Jackson had yanked his NG tube out of his nose. Jay and I panicked; we didn't know what to do but knew he could not eat without it. Therefore, off we went to our local hospital to have it reinserted.

Suffice it to say, watching them have to put that tube up his nose made me feel faint, how much longer would my baby have to endure such torment? Once we got him settled back down, we decided to let him play a bit in the paediatric toy room. Jay's phone rang and he was speaking to someone and looking at me frowning. He passed me the phone and said, "Here, you talk to her". I asked who it was and he said "Claire someone"…I didn't know anyone by that name, but took the call anyway.

She introduced herself as Claire Brownell from the Windsor Star, she had heard about our son and wanted to do a story. One of the nurses showed me to the family lounge where I could have a bit of privacy and I sat down to relay our ordeal of the last few months. We had no idea if or when the piece would be written, but sooner than we expected it hit the paper.

Well, needless to say, our first leave of absence from our new hospital proved not to be as restful or enjoyable as we had hoped and we actually longed to get back to the hospital where everything was orderly and predictable.

Chapter 21

The Stander

O nce back, after Jackson had been seen and all the initial assessments done, his daily therapy schedule began. He would have Occupational Therapy (OT), Physical Therapy (PT) and Speech and language every day. His schedule was nothing less than grueling. You have to remember, at this point, Jackson did not even have the strength to sit up. He would essentially have to learn everything all over again.

His physiotherapist, Gail Kirkwood, began with some core strengthening exercises to assist Jackson with sitting up. She would make him repeat these same exercises, much like sit ups, over and over until he could do no more. I was in tears watching him. It felt like she was torturing him.

Each day Gail would have a series of different techniques she would have him do. She told me she had never seen such a cooperative two-year-old in all her life. Once Jackson's core was strong enough, Gail worked on gaining strength in his legs. She did this by having him put in something called a stander. It was a device that Jackson's legs were velcroed into with a belt supporting him from the back. This apparatus would force him to remain in a standing position for up to 30 minutes at a time. It was the most pitiful thing you have ever seen. I could always tell when his legs were getting tired because his little bum would start bulging out of the back.

Jackson would spend thirty minutes a day in the stander in the paediatric playroom. Gail would set him up in front of a table at the correct height so that he could play games while standing. This seemed to lessen the boredom and fatigue of the experience. Little did he realize that this was all therapy.

Janet his occupational therapist would also take advantage of this time to ensure he had toys accessible that would serve the requirements of the right hand. Let me tell you, these women had a plan all figured out!

Jackson would typically do physio right after breakfast in the morning, this way he was fresh and rested. There were days however, that Gail's schedule would not permit it and Jack had to be accommodated in the afternoon. These days he was not as cooperative as she was used to. She would enter his dimly lit room during naptime and have to wake him up.

He always slept on his knees with his bum in the air, cutest thing ever! She would say "Jackson, time to do your exercises" and he would not even look at her, he would put his hand up to her face and say "no Gail, no Gail"! She would later tell us this and laugh but you could hardly blame him for not wanting to get out of bed to be tortured.

Janet Bernstein, Jackson's occupational therapist would often work with him, back to back with Gail. She was trying to help him regain the use of his right hand and arm. Janet would use simple techniques to try to encourage him to reach or grasp for objects all the while holding his left hand (now dominant) down. She was working on his fine motor skills with tasks like squeezing a ball or stringing beads.

At first, Jackson found this extremely frustrating, but slowly his brain began to adapt and he was using the right hand without conscious effort.

He began to develop a beautiful friendship with his therapists based on trust and understanding. This is not to say that my son never gave either one of them a hard time, but I think he realized they were giving him his independence back and so slowly, he began to accept this routine as a normal part of his day.

Speech and language typically followed during lunchtime. They were keeping a very close eye on his swallowing. He was still on a soft diet but at this point, the doctors felt it was safest to have him on thickened juices. They were still concerned that he could aspirate if things went down the wrong tube.

After lunch, he would go to Miss Tammy's office to practice his speech. She would often read to him and have him answer questions about the story. They would also play together and she would encourage him to respond to verbal queues. It seemed that the speech was the slowest thing to improve. We who were closest to him could understand him, but most people still could not. Even after five years, there are still times when I have to ask my son to repeat himself.

I realize that as difficult as it was to watch Jackson go through all of this, I knew it was necessary. As the days and weeks rolled by, we saw marked improvement. He was literally being transformed before our eyes. This hospital and staff were a Godsend. Once again, I want to stress how blessed we were to have access to such amazing services. Without their help, I honestly do not know where my son would be today.

Chapter 22

Beautiful Encounters

Settling in to Holland-Bloorview was easy. The staff was just an amazing group of people. If we needed anything all we had to do was go down to the family accommodations desk or ask Berta, our custodian. To call her this is simply demeaning, since she was everything to our family. This lovely woman was our hospital mother and grandmother. She provided everything from our cleaning, to fresh linens, and at times, a shoulder to cry on. There was an instant connection between her and us. When my kids saw her, Lincoln would run down the hall with arms outstretched. They would scream "Berta!" This usually brought tears to her eyes.

Berta always made a point of checking in on us, simply on a personal level. She would come by the apartment to see Jackson and check on his progress. There was a linen closet on our floor where she kept extra cleaning supplies and a few toys for the inpatient children and their families. She always had a little 'something special' for my boys. The children soon fell in love with this beautifully kind and genuine person. I think for the boys, Berta was like a grandmother. She truly gave them warmth and security during a dark time in their lives.

She was also a wonderful tailor. When we first arrived at the hospital, Jackson could not yet sit up. Berta made him a u-shaped pillow, much like a nursing pillow that we could wrap around his back to help support him while in a sitting position. She also made a Spiderman pillow for Lincoln's bed. Kindness came so naturally to her, she really was a blessing from God.

I cannot imagine what my stay would have been like without her. I looked forward to the light knock on the door, asking me if I needed anything. Sometimes I would say, "All I need is a friend". I would ask if she could stay for a short visit and I would fix us coffee and sweets. Once I learned that Berta had a sweet tooth, I tried to always have something baked or at least store bought for these occasions.

Through our chats, I would learn that she had worked at this facility for many years and had assisted hundreds of families like ours. She was always there to comfort me and offer encouragement when she sensed I was down. She would tell me to never stop praying, that God hears all of our supplications. To me Berta was the perfect addition to the Holland-Bloorview Team.

Chapter 23

Coffee Anyone?

M illey was another lovely woman we came to know. She poured our coffee every morning at Tim Horton's. She could turn a bad day around with just a smile. She had the most beautiful Jamaican accent I had ever heard. I have yet to meet anyone whose smile could instantly lift your spirits like hers. We had an immediate connection with Milley, much like we did with Berta. God put all the right people in our path to assist us through this transition.

I would invite her up to our apartment after her shift was over so we could have a visit. I would learn that she was a mother and grandmother. She had a very special touch with my boys. She knew what they liked and asked all the right questions to keep them engaged.

At Christmas, she journeyed home to Jamaica to spend the holidays with her family. Early in the New Year of 2012, there was a knock on our door. There stood Milley with Christmas gifts for all. My boys were so surprised and thrilled with their new racetrack; it kept them busy for hours. She brought Jay and me traditional gifts from Jamaica. I would often ask myself what we had done to deserve such rewards for everyone seemed to be especially kind to us.

I realize now that God never left us, not for a second. Every time we felt down or alone, He sent someone to lift our spirits. His blessings are like the sand on the seashore, endless. I can testify to His goodness, despite all that we were going through. We did not realize it then, but the events that were unfolding would alter the course of our lives. It has brought me to this point, where I can now share my son's story of courage, hope and faith.

Chapter 24

Friends through Circumstance

I recall the day I first met Billy Jo. She was sitting on a bench just outside the elevator on the second floor. Her son Brock was having his physiotherapy session. I had seen her a few times before but we only politely smiled and nodded to each other. This particular day, I decided to join her on the bench.

We instantly became friends. She had such an easy, carefree way about her and you could not help but be drawn in. So began our daily routine of chatting and getting to know each other as our boys were in therapy. Our friendship blossomed over several weeks to the point we were almost inseparable.

I invited her up to our suite so she could meet the rest of my family. I know Jay was pleased because he would soon return to work, and Lincoln would return to school at home, leaving Jackson and I to ride out the last six weeks together.

Our boys were roughly the same age and although they had different diagnosis, they both had mobility issues. The kids got along as well as we did . It was a perfect fit. While they played on the floor with cars and trucks, she and I would watch TV and hang out. This quickly became our new routine every evening from Monday to Thursday. I would learn that Billy Jo had three other children at home and a husband. Every Friday to Sunday she was granted a leave to go home to the rest of her family. Unfortunately, for us, we were four hours from home, so leaves only happened once a month.

People can say they understand what you are going through, but from one mother to another, Billy Jo and I would beg to differ. We would confide in each other and voice our fears about what the future would look like for our boys. As a parent, you always want your children's lives to be easy. You do not want to see them struggle, let alone be different or ostracized. Society can be cruel, let alone for someone that does not fit the 'norm'.

I have prayed to God that my son would be accepted and that He would open doors of opportunity for him. I do worry at times that he may be bullied or teased, but I am trying to teach him that his physical body is only a shell, that the real Jackson is on the inside. I told him that God does not make mistakes, He made you just the way He wanted you to be. He has plans for your future and you are perfect in His eyes.

At times, Billy Jo and I just had to get out of the hospital. We needed to feel that there was still a real, normal life out there somewhere.

We would not go out for long, but even to do groceries was a treat. As we walked up and down the aisles, we would often ask each other; "Do you think anyone could guess what we're going through right now? Do you think we look any different?" The answer to these questions is no. We looked just like everyone else. Life was still going on around us, despite our circumstances. People would have no idea that we were living in a hospital with our kids.

This was our new reality. It was now normal for us to push our sons around in wheelchairs and experience the stares of gawkers. If people only knew how far each of them had come, or what they had been through up to that point, they would hang their heads in shame.

In the safety of the hospital, among the best doctors and therapists in the country, we knew we were giving our children the best possible chance they had. In a matter of a few short weeks, Billy Jo became one of the best friends I ever had. I truly do not know that I could have made it through that last stretch without her.

Certainly, the boys grew close and began to depend on each other for companionship and support.

I have come to realize that through this whole experience, God has sent us just what we needed and at the exact moment. As difficult as it has been, God has rained down so many blessings on my family it is hard to look back on any of it with regret. I would of course never want to see my child suffer the way he did, but when I look back on all that God has done during and since, I would not change a thing. This is Jackson's journey, his destiny, foretold by our Heavenly Father, the rest of us have merely been given our roles to play in it.

Chapter 25

Front Page News

T he phone started ringing, first family, then friends and neighbours; asking if we had seen the front page of today's paper. No, I say as I make my way to the mailbox. This happened to be on a weekend that we were on leave from the hospital.

As I pull the newspaper out of the mailbox, there was our family on the front page of The Windsor Star. The headline read, "Tot, 2, suffers rare paediatric stroke". Even though I remember giving the interview and doing the photo shoot, when you see yourself in the paper it is still a bit surreal. There was something about seeing our life in print and shared with the world that really seemed to solidify it for me. Even though we were living this nightmare, it felt like a bit of a dream; as if we would someday wake up and realize this could not be happening to us.

It was shortly after the article came out that the letters and cards started pouring in. How people even knew where we lived was a mystery to me, yet somehow these encouraging notes kept finding their way into our mailbox. One in particular stood out from the rest. It came from a perfect stranger, an elderly man who was in a retirement home.

He had read the story in the paper and felt compelled to reach out to us. He himself had felt the devastating effects of a stroke. In his letter, he shared the highs and lows of his experience and told us that he was praying for our son and wishing him a full and speedy recovery.

I have often thought of this man over the years and wondered how he is doing. I always said that I would bring Jackson to meet him but somehow we have never made it there. I realize now that he could simply have been one of God's messengers sent to us in our hour of need. Some people say God works in mysterious ways, but I say He does all things according to His will.

Every encounter with someone, every hardship we face, is a test to help us grow in our spiritual journey. These experiences mold and shape us, ultimately defining our divine destinies, all of which are preordained by God.

Even my son's stroke, as awful as the whole experience was, I would not change it. We have been highly favored by God as a result and the blessings we have received are too numerous to count. Now that I have embraced this, I have finally been able to make peace with it. My son is not a victim; he is blessed!

Chapter 26

Progress

"Look Mommy!" Jackson called out as he came barrelling down the hallway of the second floor with Gail his physiotherapist jogging behind him to catch up. Jackson had been learning to ride again.

The little red tricycle looked like any ordinary bike with the exception that this one had been adapted with extra safety belts and foot clips to ensure he would not fall off. This bike riding was now part of his regular exercise routine to strengthen his gross motor skills as well as his balance.

Being on a bike gave Jackson a newfound sense of freedom, something he had not had in over three months. When he was riding through the halls of the hospital, he was so happy and he looked like your typical toddler. These moments were often the highlight of my days. We had now been in hospital over five months and truthfully, it was starting to take a toll on me.

On the days that I was feeling down, Jackson would always seem to have a breakthrough. God knew that I needed picking up. Those were the days that He carried me. I slowly watched God take my crippled son and with the help of these amazing therapists, give him his life back. Jackson was literally being transformed before our eyes.

For those who do not believe in the power of prayer, let me be a witness. When my son was in the Intensive Care Unit, clinging to life, all we could do was pray. God heard our prayers, and my son came out of the ICU. We continued in prayer and a couple of months later, he could talk again, and then walk again.

Here we are now, five years later and I have a typical seven-year-old boy who loves cars and bike riding. The difference between Jackson, besides his physical limitations, is that God has touched him. He has been to Heaven and sees angels. God chose him for this divine journey.

In my daily talks with The Father, I have asked Him why he chose my son, why our family? Then I realize that we are all God's children, and He will use us any way He wants or needs to get out His message. This is Jackson's story of hope and courage, which I bring to you my readers. I offer you a glimpse of Heaven through the eyes of my child.

Chapter 27

RMH and the Canadian Open

I was at work. It was a typical day like any other, when I received an email from an unexpected source. The email was an invitation sent from the Ronald McDonald House Charities Canada, to attend the Canadian Open at Glen Abbey Golf Club. We were invited to spend the day representing families who had used the house and benefitted from its amenities. To be asked was quite an honor and we were very excited about this opportunity. This was not our first engagement for the house, we had done a few speaking engagements prior. We felt it was our responsibility to let our community know just how much this organization does for families in their time of need.

I felt so blessed to be able to give back in this way. It was an opportunity to open doors for RMH each time we were asked to speak and share our story. Each person who came to the house during our time there left changed. People always said to me, "I never knew, I had no idea that all this was available to families." I myself never knew, until I was there. You never think something like this will affect your family, until it does. RMH slogan is "Helping give sick children what they need most...their families."

I can attest to how true this statement is. You cannot be there emotionally for your sick child if you have to worry about bills or where you will eat or sleep. The RMH was our beacon light on a very dark corner. I will always remember how they showed us love and compassion when our world was crashing down around us. The friendships that we formed while there will be for a lifetime. God was there for us through it all. He gave us so much joy, love, and a peace that I carry with me still today. I have come to realize that this experience has made our entire family better in every way. It has shaped us all and put us on our divine paths.

The day arrived when we attended the Open and we were greeted by an escort who showed us the royal treatment. We were all given VIP passes and a guided tour of the club. They led us to the RMH tent that was set up with a putting green, photo layout booth, and lots of free merchandise. Both of my boys were given a new set of golf clubs and we had a mock photo shoot for Golf Digest Magazine. Let me tell you, my husband looked like a pro on the cover! Cathy, the CEO of RMH

Canada, led us as we toured the green and watched in silent awe, while the best players in North America competed for the title.

We had a lavish lunch in the Clubhouse Loft Suites and mingled with the golfers. It was at a time like this I wish I had followed the sport a little closer! After lunch, we went to a trailer that looked like mission control. This was where it all happened. The game was televised so once inside we were asked to remain quiet. The cameras were on every hole and there must have been 30 televisions on all at the same time, capturing every shot and every angle. All the major networks were there to catch minute-by-minute plays. Jackson was allowed to sit down at the main control panel wearing the directors head set for a picture. This was definitely one of the coolest experiences I have ever had.

The day was over before we knew it, poor Jackson was so worn out that he fell asleep in his stroller. Even as we made our way to our car a marketing person stopped us and the boys were each given an auto-graphed Bubba Watling visor. This just topped off a fantastic day! It was just another example of God's blessings raining down on us, letting each of us know there is always a silver lining.

Chapter 28
Recollections

Sept 9, 2014

J ackson has mentioned things about heaven over the last couple of years, however his accounts seen to be getting more detailed and he's bringing them up more often.

Tonight after a rough day with his asthma, I was lying with him and he began talking about the boy who died in the hospital and went to heaven. He was referring to the boy in the movie 'Heaven is for Real'. I told him the boy went to heaven while the doctors were working on him in the operating room. Jackson became upset and told me he didn't want to go back to heaven. He wanted to stay here with his family. I told him he wasn't going anywhere, that God has special plans for him.

I asked Jackson if he'd met God and he said no. He talked about Jesus being a man, and I also asked him what heaven looked like and he said "angels are flying everywhere and praising Jesus and God and singing". I asked him "Do they have hair?" He said "no, they are all just bright and sparkly, their wings sparkle."

Jackson also said "Heaven is all golden brown color." At this point we changed the subject and I asked him if he remembered being in my tummy as a baby. He told me "yes, Lincoln was on top and I was on the bottom. His butt was in my face!"

While pregnant with Lincoln, I was expecting twins but had a fall down the stairs and began to bleed. When I had an ultrasound, the doctors detected both sacs but only one heartbeat. This makes me wonder, could Jackson be the baby I lost come back? Could his soul have been born again three years later? Makes me wonder…

He then asked me "Mommy, does it hurt to be born?" I told him I didn't think so, at this point, he rolled over and went right to sleep.

Chapter 29

Blessings from a Stranger

One week-night, about a month into our stay at Holland-Bloorview Children's Hospital, Jay decided that he would go out and get pizza for supper. Unlike in our hometown of Windsor, which is renowned for the best pizza in the country, we were hard pressed to find a locally owned pizzeria. Therefore, we settled on Pizza Pizza. While standing in line, a woman behind him asked if he was from Windsor. "Yes I am, how did you know"? She said, "I noticed your Spitfires jacket, I am also from Windsor." The Windsor Spitfires are our local hockey team. This struck up a conversation between my husband and a perfect stranger.

While they waited for their order, this woman asked Jay what brought him to Toronto. So, he told our story start to finish and by the time they left the restaurant, they were both in tears. She hugged him tenderly from one parent to another, understanding the immense pain he was in.

She told Jay that she often gets tickets through her work for different sporting events and asked if he could use a night out. By this time we had been in hospital for nearly fifteen weeks. He told her sure and gave her the name of where we were staying. She said she would drop them off next week.

True to her word, the following week, she came by the hospital with an envelope addressed to Jay. It was around eleven o'clock, Jackson had completed his morning therapy sessions and Jay and I were back in our suite. The phone rang in our room; it was reception telling us that we had a visitor. I was busy getting Lincoln ready for school, he went daily from 11:30-2:30, and so Jay went downstairs to see who could possibly be here to see us.

When I came home from dropping Lincoln at school, I found Jay upstairs in our suite. His eyes were puffy and he handed me an envelope. I asked him "What's wrong"? He said, "Just open it", and so I did. Within moments, I too was crying. I absolutely could not believe what I was reading. The woman that Jay had met at the pizzeria was in fact a lawyer, and she and her husband adopt a family every year at Christmas and this year, they chose us as their family. Enclosed within the Christmas card, were four tickets to a hockey game and a cheque for $500. She had written a beautiful note of encouragement, and asked us to have a wonderful Christmas for our children.

God had once again brought angels into our lives. We had no time to think about Christmas, let alone shopping or putting up a tree. At this point, we did not even know if Jackson would have a leave from the hospital to be able to go home for the holidays.

The money from these generous people, allowed us to put a few gifts under the Christmas tree and make my children feel that Santa had not forgotten them.

We sent pictures and a thank you card and promised to keep in touch. Not long into the New Year, we got a call from her asking us if we would like to go to their home for dinner.

Chapter 30
Unlikely Friendships

We pulled up in the driveway of a newly modern home in a beautiful old neighborhood. Her husband greeted us at the door with a warm and genuine smile. Standing in the wings were two adorable little girls.

It felt great to get out of the hospital setting and feel like regular people. This was our old life, which seemed like a distant memory now. We had been living in hospitals so long now it was beginning to feel normal to us.

Wonderful smells were coming from the kitchen, which was a lovely open concept room. Our host was already preparing the sides while her husband had the barbecue warming up on the back patio. It did not matter that there was a foot of snow outside. My mouth watered just thinking about a steak in the winter. This is what we would be doing if we were at home, but instead we were eating thrown together meals in a dreary communal kitchen on the sixth floor of a hospital ward.

You could tell this was a happy home; it had a very inviting feel to it. The children seemed a bit unsure of one another at the beginning but they quickly overcame their shyness and had a very enjoyable time together.

It was good for Jackson to be around children his own age who were not challenged. All the children that he was exposed to at the hospital had special needs. Not that this was a bad thing, not at all. It taught my son empathy, first hand. I do however want him to go through life feeling normal, and not limited in any way. I often wonder if Jackson sees himself as a special needs child. He certainly attempts most things and wants to be just like everyone else. He always pushes himself and has a zest for life!

We sat down to dinner together, two families, from completely different walks of life. We had crossed paths through divine intervention.

We truly had an enjoyable evening, mingling with these lovely people. Once again, God planted these people in our path who He knew we needed at that exact moment. Each step of this journey we were on with our son, brought us more and more blessings.

Chapter 31

Fitting in

I cannot tell you how hard it has been over these last four years, watching my son try to fit it. We thought there was a lot of awareness about disabilities, but when faced with it head on, we realized the extent of ignorance that was still out there. You expect stares from children, but from adults, it is still upsetting. I would rather people approach me and ask me what happened to my son so I can explain the devastating effects of stroke.

My son walks with a noticeable limp, and his right arm has a tendency to hang while his hand is fisted. He is also overweight because he has a healthy appetite but limited mobility. All of these factors combined just seem to make him attractive to gawkers.

I can share with you a perfect example of how a day of fun spent with supposed friends turned out to be an emotional disaster.

It was during summer vacation of 2015, I had made plans with two friends and their children to go to the zoo. This local zoo also had a splash pad, lots of climbing structures, picnic areas, and many other fun things to do. We had just got there and unloaded our vehicles when the children spied the jungle gym located outside the main entrance. They immediately ran over to it and proceeded to play. Meanwhile, it takes me some time to get Jackson out of the van, into his stroller and grab all of our stuff. Not once did either of my friends ask me if I needed any help.

By the time I get Jackson over to the play structure, he wants to try to climb the rock wall. I would have preferred he use the stairs, but he keeps pushing himself to try new things, so I go with it. I stand behind him, helping him put one foot up at a time. By the time he reached the top, I was pooped! He was so proud of himself; his smile made it all worth it.

Just when he decided to go over to have some fun with the kids, they all jump off the structure and decide they are ready to go to see the animals. My son and I are left standing atop the jungle gym watching the entire group walk away from us, my oldest son included. Just a few nights earlier, I had to remind Lincoln to always include his brother when these same kids had been over to our house and none of them would play with Jackson. Just then, Lincoln turns around and says,

"Mom, are you coming?" I say you go on, I'll stay here with Jack, as I begin to cry. Somehow, I already knew the day would go like this.

Well, just then, Lincoln starts running back to us. He climbs up the play structure, sits down next to Jack, puts his arm around his brother and begins to cry. I was never so proud of my son for standing up for what's right. He also has had a very tough road. He lost a bit of his childhood through this ordeal as well. He has had to witness things children should not have to see. We also rely on him a lot to help us with Jackson. The strength of his character was never as evident as it was in that moment.

The rest of the group finally realized that they left us behind and came walking back. To be honest, I think my friends were a bit embarrassed and perhaps ashamed by their behaviour. They made a comment that we came together, so we will all stay together. Well, I can tell you that did not last long. By lunchtime, they ditched us again and had lunch without us.

I spent the entire day alone with my sons. My so-called friends did not spend more than five minutes with me all day. So much for other mothers understanding and compassion.

The highlight of Jackson's day was while playing in the sandbox, this sweet little girl named Emily came to join him to build a sand castle. She never asked any questions, never gave him any stares, and just accepted him as he is. In that moment, God sent us this perfect little angel. I sent up my thanks. Someone once told me "prayers go up and blessings come down" and it has never failed me yet.

To make my point, other than sweet Emily, not one child approached my son all day to play. Jackson even said, "Why does everyone hate me?" Parents need to start educating their children about differences. So-called "normal" kids, need to realize that differences in others are okay. That we are all created uniquely beautiful. After all, isn't it what's on the inside that counts? We are all guilty of judging others, of making assumptions, but I myself try not to do that anymore, for you never know what someone else is going through.

We are so wrapped up in our own lives, so busy with our own commitments that we truly do not see what is around us, nor do we take the time to care enough about others. This goes against God's own rules for us to live by. We are supposed to love others as ourselves, but so seldom do I ever witness this in everyday life. We all need to start living our lives with purpose and meaning. We need to live heaven culture right here on earth.

Chapter 32

Sacrifices of Love

L et me not forget to talk about the sacrifices my then five year old had to make. Lincoln was only in Senior Kindergarten when his brother became ill. He lost his childhood and was forced to grow up way too fast. This family tragedy affected us all in different ways.

When we first headed off to London Hospital, we had little time to think. All we knew was that it was life and death for Jackson. We scarcely had time to consider what all this meant to Lincoln. He was the big brother left behind. In our minds, we were doing the right thing by keeping him at home hoping he felt safe and secure. Lord knows Jay and I were out of our minds with worry and fear. We truly believed that by leaving Lincoln behind, he would somehow be unaffected. How wrong we turned out to be.

Our poor little big man had to endure counselling in school because of his pent up feelings. The teachers would find him sitting in a corner by himself staring out the window. He became introverted and angry. He was bounced around from our house to the neighbours, to Grandma's, he probably didn't know if he was coming or going. The one thing he did know was that his family seemed to have abandoned him.

I am sure he was scared, and probably wondered if we were coming back. Lincoln became lost in the chaos of it all. He had to take a back seat to the needs of his brother; his best friend and playmate that he scarcely recognized now...

Our friends and family over compensated to help him through this rough patch. We would later see photos of him eating chocolate and washing it down with a big gulp of milk! He was shown extra love and attention, had many sleepovers and playdates to help him take his mind off things.

One of my favorite memories was of our friends Nick and Diane taking Lincoln to a Halloween place called BOO. Diane would later have a whole roll of film for me, which contained the adventures of that day. Looking at my son in those photos, he seemed so happy, as if he did not have a care in the world. For the first time since our ordeal began, he looked just like a typical five year old, having fun. I will always be grateful to those friends and family that helped look out for him in a time that was so uncertain in his life.

Chapter 33

The School at the Top of the Hill

B ecause the last three months of his life were so unstable, we decided that we needed to go to Toronto as a family. There would be no leaving anyone behind. We enrolled Lincoln in the Toronto District School board and so he had to say goodbye to his friends, teachers, and all that was familiar.

As we walked up the steps of this very old school, we were all a bit apprehensive. This was a scary, yet exciting time for Lincoln. We followed the signs to the office where we had a meeting scheduled with the principal. A rather tall woman came out to greet us wearing blue jeans and running shoes. She shook our hands and introduced herself as such. We were a bit shocked by her casual attire but pleasantly surprised by the warmth that exuded from her. During our meeting, several students walked in and out of her office at their leisure and she knew each child by name. We instinctively knew Lincoln would be in good hands here.

As we made our way to the Junior Kindergarten/ Senior Kindergarten classroom to meet Lincoln's new teacher, I vividly remember him giving my hand a tight squeeze and looking up at me for reassurance. I told him all would be ok, and besides, he would have a grand adventure to share with his friends and classmates when we returned home.

We were introduced to his new teacher, Mr. Zamora. He was a petite Asian man with a great big smile. He had been briefed on the new student and therefore knew Lincoln needed to be treated with kid gloves. He readily took him under his wing and showed him around. After introducing Lincoln to the class, he went over the schedule for the week and told us to have him report the next day.

We chose the daily afternoon schedule for him, which was 11:30 to 2:30. We figured this would give him good consistency and still allow us to attend most of Jackson's therapy sessions. As it turned out, while Lincoln was at school, Jackson was usually napping which allowed my husband and me a bit of time to ourselves. Life seemed to be getting into a routine, however unusual it was.

And so, the days wore on and we all adjusted to our new home and schedules. Lincoln had begun to settle into his new school and even made a friend named Oliver. This little boy had recently also moved to Toronto, and so the two new kids had found each other. I thanked God every day for Oliver because Lincoln found the children here to be quite different from back home and was having a hard time fitting in.

Mr. Zamora also took Lincoln under his wing; he knew he had been through an awful lot emotionally. One afternoon when I picked him up from school, Mr. Zamora called me aside to brief me on Lincoln's progress. It was mostly positive, although he said he did have some days that he was quite sad and distant. The teacher was very touched by my son's affectionate nature. He said, "Your son is so affectionate, he always thanks me at the end of the day and gives me a hug." When I asked Lincoln how his day was, he said to me "Mom, Mr. Zamora says I'm a hugger!" To which I laughed out loud, I had never heard that expression before.

The SK class was working on a Christmas celebration and the parents were welcome to come for the event. As Jay and I filed in among the other parents, we felt a bit like outsiders in this place. People here were definitely not warm and fuzzy like we were used to back home. Many of the children were dropped off at school by their nanny, definitely a foreign concept for us in Windsor.

As the children took their places, Mr. Zamora led them in song. He was not only an amazing teacher, but also a wonderful vocalist! They sang all the traditional Christmas songs, and our Lincoln, one of the tallest kids, was beaming with pride from the back row. Looking at him there, in that moment, I knew that our first-born was going to be all right. We were all going to come through this, a little tougher, definitely stronger, but we would come out on the other side. Thanks be to God, for He gave us all the strength that we needed during the toughest ordeal of our lives.

Chapter 34

The Stairway to Heaven

Journal Entry:
September 9, 2014

I asked him if angels are boys or girls and he said "all girls". I asked, "Do they have hair?" he said, "No, they are all just bright and sparkly. Their wings sparkle." He said, "Heaven is all golden brown color."

I believed Jackson when he said that he had been to heaven. However, the one thing he never described in much detail was the encounter he had with my father "Grandpa Eddie." A lovely woman named Veronica Green, a spiritual medium had described to me what that encounter looked like.

I pulled up to a quaint little blue home surrounded by a white picket fence. I immediately thought that this must be to keep the good spirits in and the bad ones out! I am not too sure what I had expected Veronica to look like, but she was lovely and had the most amazing eyes I had ever seen. When they say that the eyes are the windows to the soul, they weren't kidding, I felt like she knew all of my deepest secrets with just one look.

I patiently waited while she prepared the room, lighting the white candles and preparing herself mentally for my read. I waited with anticipation for what was to come. I had never been to see a medium before and frankly, I wasn't sure if I believed in them.

As soon as I was seated across from this lovely woman, I felt as though she could see into my soul. She immediately began to tell me things about me that she could have never have known. She stared at me with such intensity that I could not even look away.

She began to describe my life in vivid detail; she knew I had two boys, a husband and a dog I had recently lost. Wow, I thought to myself, she is the real deal.

There was something so intimate about this read. She told me things about myself that made me laugh or just nod in assent. I felt like I could share my innermost secrets with this total stranger. This made me realize another beautiful thing about God; He uses people and situations to get through to us. I recorded my read with Veronica, and here are a few excerpts:

Veronica told me that my son Lincoln is highly gifted. She told me that he can "see". She asked me if he ever talks about people that have passed on.

She said that Jackson came through in the reading as a baby. He told Veronica that he had pain and cramping in his legs. He also had pain in his head. He had trouble rolling over when he was little. Veronica suspects that there may have been something wrong with Jackson when he was 10 months old. He was pointing to his head because he had headaches.

Veronica's account of Jackson's encounter with Grandpa Eddie: He saw his grandfather; your baby can see on the other side, he communicates with those on the other side. He has had an experience.

You never met the child you lost, it's a girl, you lost a girl....(While pregnant with Lincoln, I was carrying twins and had a fall down the stairs, resulting in the death of one of the fetus') you are going to find that your younger son has traits of your daughter. She has long beautiful hair, its reddish blonde, white skin and she says "hi mommy". This is why you feel the presence of a girl around you, it's your daughter, and she's always with you.

Grandpa is the one who made him come back. Mommy needs you, he said. Did he tell you about the stairs? He went to the top of the stairs and Grandpa was in the bedroom.

Chapter 35
The Benefit

W hile still in London hospital, we discovered that friends of my husband were secretly planning a benefit for us. When we found out, neither of us felt right about it. We have always been independent people, and having to ask others for help was not something either of us was comfortable with.

When his friends explained to us how everyone felt so helpless, we figured that this benefit would allow them to feel they were doing something to contribute to our cause. These were wonderfully giving people that my husband worked with. Most of these Chrysler workers knew my husband for nearly 25 years.

Within a matter of a few short weeks, what they pulled off was simply amazing...

They canvassed local businesses throughout the city for raffle prizes. What they received in exchange for our story was outstanding. It included everything from a big screen TV, to a wine fridge, autographed hockey jerseys, gift certificates and the list goes on. Let me not forget to mention that a local hall donated the use of their facility and all the food for our event. We had a wonderful pasta dinner with all the trimmings.

Lincoln's classmates had decorated a huge banner, which his teachers mounted over the food area. Each child in his class decorated it with a sentimental Christmas picture and words of encouragement. They clearly missed their friend and classmate.

His two teachers also made up a jar of jellybeans and turned it into a guessing game for which they sold tickets. Once again, all of the money collected was for us.

As we entered the hall, we saw that plenty of people had arrived before us. We were welcoming our guests when my husband tapped me on the shoulder. He said, "look over there", and when I did, all I saw were the faces of our RMH friends that had made the drive down from London to be there for us. These parents had left the bedside of their sick child to be there to support us. Needless to say, Jay and I could not stop the flow of tears.

There were people from my work, Jay's work, friends, neighbours, family, church members, and some people we had not seen in years. After 600, we stopped counting. Apparently, there was a lineup outside that wrapped around the building. The fire chief told the hall owner that we were well over capacity and refused to let anyone else in. Therefore, when the announcement was made to the people outside, these amazing individuals were not discouraged; they simply ordered takeout food and left a monetary donation at the door.

Each person that entered the benefit that night was an angel sent from God. Not only was the money going to come in handy, but more importantly, each person touched us in a very special and unique way. They all filled us with hope and love.

As I looked around the room in that moment, all the fear and uncertainty vanished. I knew that no matter the outcome, we had a whole community here to support us. After a truly blessed evening, we left that place with renewed hope and faith that our family was going to be all right.

Chapter 36

Transitioning Home

I t was now 200 days or 6 months and 18 days since
our ordeal began. One would think I would be thrilled
to be home. So why could I not stop crying? I walk
around my home aimlessly pining for the one bedroom
apartment that we occupied in the hospital.

Life was so simple there, so routine and ever so safe.
Perhaps it was having the proximity to the doctors and
nurses that I found so reassuring. After all, there were
no code blue buttons on our walls at home. All future
incidents would be mine to manage with no formal CPR
training. Let me tell you, watching your child choke and
not knowing what to do is the most helpless feeling in
the world.

Unfortunately, I had to have a crash course in CPR,
certainly not ever the way I had hoped to learn. I had
to dial 911 on more than one occasion. I often wonder

the long-term effects on Lincoln for having to witness these events.

Jay kept asking me why I was crying. "Aren't you glad to be home?" To be honest, I really could not explain it. I was happy to be home with family and friends for support, however the hospital life had become our new normal, it had started to feel almost like a new life. I realize this must sound bizarre, but truly, I cannot explain all the emotions I was feeling at the time.

I realize now that I was suffering from post-traumatic stress. For all those months, Jay and I had to be strong for Jackson. He was turning to us for his emotional support and strength. I am sure my son feels that he got his courage from us, but let me tell you, no greater courage have I ever witnessed than what my son displayed. He was just a baby, and when I think back on all that he went through, I honestly do not think most adults would have fared nearly as well or been half as brave as he was.

I was so glad to be reunited with my dog again. I always say Cisko was my first child; we got the dog first as a dry run, to try out parenting in a way! I had missed my best friend and I could tell he sure missed me too. He was apprehensive for the first week or so; I suspect he kept thinking we were going to leave again. We resumed our walks, although with Jackson back in a stroller, so we took a much more leisurely pace than what he was used to.

Life slowly got into a routine, although it certainly did not resemble anything close to what it used to be. In total, I was away from work for nearly 14 months. I guess a part of me was also mourning the life I had which for the moment seemed lost. Life was carrying on all around me and yet there was a time it felt like it was standing still. My friends and coworkers were carrying on with their life and a bitter part of me resented them for that.

I remember feeling angry a lot. I was very disappointed in my family and friends who for some reason (in my own twisted mind) felt that now that we were home, our life was somehow normal again. Few people called or stopped by, let alone offered to help us or even watch the kids so Jay and I could have some time for ourselves. My psychologist told me I needed to ask for help, "People don't want to impose, you must ask them for the help, and let them know what you need." This upset me because I felt that they should know we were worn out emotionally, we should not have to ask.

It took a few counselling sessions for me to come to terms with everything. At the root of it all, I believe everyone was afraid to watch Jackson because of everything he went through. It made people nervous to have to be responsible for him, even if it was just for a couple of hours. This is why Jay and I agreed to send him to The John McGivney Children's Centre when it was time for me to return to work. This facility dealt with children with varying degrees of disabilities. I knew that I could resume working knowing that Jackson was in a safe and structured environment.

All those feelings are behind me now, I do not hold grudges, and I realize that everyone has a busy life trying to juggle full time work with a home and children. I do very much appreciate those people in my life who stepped up to help, who held me up when I needed it or just let me cry when I could do nothing else. You all know who you are and I am forever in your debt.

Chapter 37

The Entity

Journal Entry:

May 22, 2015

Something woke me around 3am and I sat bolt upright up in bed. I heard voices coming from down the hall. I walked towards Jackson's room and stood outside his bedroom door. I could hear loud whispering coming from inside. When I threw open the door, Jackson was, sound asleep.

We had come to realize that something was happening with Jackson. Something or someone was trying to communicate with him from the other side. One night while reading him a story, (he was around 4 years old at the time) he pointed to the corner of his bedroom and said "Mommy, tell him to go away". Immediately, I looked over to where he was pointing, and as the hairs stood up on the back of my neck, I said, "Who honey"? "Him, over there, tell him to go away, he's bugging me".

I told him that I did not see anyone there but he kept insisting. I suggested that we finish our story since it was almost bedtime. After I put him to bed, I told Jay what he had said and neither of us could believe it. Were the angels he had been talking about trying to come through to him? We didn't know what to make of it...

Things seemed to quiet down after this and I rarely gave it any more thought until strange and unexplained things began to happen. Jackson had begun to wake up in the middle of the night. Every night something was waking him up between 3:00 and 4:30 am. I would go into his room to find him sitting up in bed crying and scared. When I would ask him what was wrong, he would tell me "something woke me up".

Night after night, we would have the same reoccurrence. He would always tell me the same thing, "something keeps waking me up". I finally asked him, "something or someone?"

He said "the ghost". I will not lie; this frightened me, but intrigued me at the same time. This is something that you see in the movies. When I asked Jackson what the ghost looked like, I expected him to say, like an angel, or bright and white, but instead he said "like a black shadow". Ok, this scared me, it did not sound like a friendly ghost. I knew we had to do something about this.

He began to ask me to keep a night light on in his room, specifically in the one corner of his room he always referred to as "the dark corner." This is where he would see the ghost, always in the same corner of his room next to his dresser.

So began my nightly prayer vigil for my son. I felt like he was under attack. Satan knew my son was special, touched by God and He wanted him. I would pray that he be surrounded by God's loving light and that his guardian angels would watch over him through the night. I took to leaving his bedroom door open as well so I could hear even the slightest sound during the night.

They call children like Jackson, children of the light, or rainbow children. If he truly is, I will never know for sure, but one thing I do know is that he is special. God has a calling on my son's life and perhaps in some way, I am supposed to help him fulfill it.

Chapter 38

The Spirit in the room

S trange things kept happening in our home, but mostly in Jackson's room. Lights would always brighten and dim, this was routine by now. However, one thing I will never forget was Jackson asking me to turn on his fish tank light. He was afraid that night and he wanted his room lit up. As I walked towards his dresser, his television came on all by itself. I wheeled around because I could not believe what just happened. I looked at Jack, he looked at me and I said, "Maybe it was Grandpa Eddie"? He smiled and said "yeah, maybe".

There was another time when he asked for a night light and all of a sudden, his fish tank came on all on its own. We began to get used to these things and were not afraid until he began waking up in the night again, frightened. He would tell me he heard strange noises from the dark corner.

I had heard of a local businessman who did home inspections with thermal imaging. Someone that I work with had shown me an image that this person took while doing a home inspection in an older neighborhood. It was a full-blown image of a ghost standing in front of a stove in the kitchen. I was speechless when I saw it; never did I imagine that such technology could capture something like this until he came to our house.

After showing my husband the image of the ghost, he placed a call to this man and he came to inspect our house a few days later. To our shock and amazement, he captured an image of a ghost sitting on our sofa in the basement. I will tell you, it was a bit unsettling. However, this explained a lot concerning Jackson. If our son was in fact tuned into a higher spiritual frequency, it made sense that this spirit was somehow trying to connect with him.

We needed to figure out if it was positive or negative energy being displayed by the ghost. Why was our son afraid? Who is it? These were only some of the questions we were asking ourselves.

As Jay and I tried to figure out who could be haunting our home, the logical explanation kept pointing to the original homeowner. We knew when we purchased the house that there had been a death, but it was natural causes. This never bothered either of us, people die in their homes all the time, it does not mean that the spirit will go on to haunt the home.

We inquired with some of our neighbours and to our surprise, some of them told us that the original owner died of a heart attack in the kitchen, while others told us he had shot himself in the bedroom. How could these stories be so vastly different? I was puzzled, until my husband revealed a secret from nearly 11 years ago.

When we purchased our home, Jay knew he would do significant renovations to it. The first order of the day would be to change out the hardwood floors. While tearing out the old flooring, he came across a huge stain in what is now Jackson's room. He said it looked like blood that had seeped right through the carpet to the sub flooring. Ironically, enough, besides the basement family room, Jack's bedroom was the only other room to have carpeting and we wondered why. We began to put it all together, and we suspect there may have been a murder in our son's room. This would explain the stain, the ghost, the strange occurrences; it all made sense.

It was now time to call in a professional. I phoned Veronica Green, and asked her if she had ever cleared a house? Yes, she had done some successfully and so we thought it time to put the ghost to rest.

Chapter 39

The Clearing

We anxiously awaited the arrival of Veronica and her husband Mike. They had agreed to help clear our house of this unwanted presence. I certainly did not know what to expect, all I had ever seen about this topic was movies like the exorcist and that scared me to death!

Regardless of how we felt, Jay and I knew we had to do this for Jackson. It was starting to take a toll on him. He was anxious around bedtime, not wanting to go to sleep. One of us always had to lay with him each night until he fell asleep. Then because he was waking up in the middle of the night, consistently, he would be so tired at school, sometimes falling asleep in class or even outside during recess. We knew we had to at least try to get him some help. I am not sure that either of us was convinced this would work.

They began by doing a walkthrough of our home. First, the main floor, then they moved upstairs. Room by room, all seemed well, and then Veronica crossed the threshold to Jackson's room. She immediately put her hand to her chest and said she was having difficulty breathing. She asked me if I could feel it. Feel what, I asked. "The cold", she said. Thank God, I couldn't feel it. Veronica then asked us for white candles. "We must surround ourselves with the white light of the Holy Spirit" she said. It was at this point that Jay got spooked and left the room.

After closing the bedroom door and the blinds, she lit the candles and was ready to begin. She immediately walked over to his dresser and studied the wall behind it. She asked me what if anything was behind that wall. I told her only Lincoln's bedroom closet.

She felt the presence in that corner of the room. She said the energy was dark and not good. I told her this was always the corner Jackson was afraid of, 'the dark corner'.

As she began to say a prayer, Mike was sprinkling holy water on the wall. Veronica's eyes got really wide and I asked her what was happening. She said, "He doesn't want to leave; he feels that he's protecting your son."

As she was communicating with this entity, I could clearly see the struggle she was having. Her eyes were closed, however I could see her eyeballs twitching constantly through closed lids. She was waving her hands back and forth and telling it to go to the light.

Suddenly, her eyes flew open and the look on her face resembled fear or perhaps shock. She said the ghost had first appeared as an older man but as she insisted that it leave our home, it transformed before her eyes. She said it stood very tall, and black wings protruded from its back. Its mouth was open and it was making something like a hissing sound. She said part of its face was missing on the one side and most of its teeth.

She did feel that this person had his face shot off as we suspected, this would explain the pool of dried blood that my husband found when he pulled the carpeting up.

The spirit kept insisting to Veronica that he did not take his own life. He said that he had an argument with a friend and there was drinking and shouting and he was shot as a result. She said she could go deeper and find out what happened or she could just clear our home, so she and I agreed we needed to help Jackson and not open Pandora's Box.

In hindsight, Jay and I wish we had asked more questions; perhaps we could have helped solve a cold case and given closure to a family. I have made my peace with this, knowing that Veronica helped this lost soul find his way to heaven. Jay still harbours regret and says he will always live with the fact he never found out who it was that died in our house. He feels that we did the spirit an injustice by not delving deeper.

Chapter 40

Voices

"Mommy, do you hear that?"
"Hear what?" I ask,
"That beautiful heaven music".

After Veronica cleared our home, we had no more events. We thought everything was ok since Jackson seemed so much more peaceful and no longer troubled. Then one night, months later, at bedtime, the following conversation between him and I took place:

Journal Entry: 01/06/2016

As I tuck Jackson into bed, I lay down with him, as is my custom. I was weary; it had been a long day. My son gets unusually chatty at bedtime; meanwhile I long for the quiet of night. No sooner had I rolled over on to my side, I drifted right to sleep.

"Mommy, do you hear that"? As I struggled to draw myself out of sleep, I ask him "hear what"? He says "the lady walking down the hall in her high heeled shoes". I say, "No honey, I don't hear it". He says, "Mom, you don't hear her walking?" Again, I tell him no. He says, "You know those shoes with the sticks on the back of them? It sounds like she rolled the carpet up in our hallway and was walking in those kinds of shoes". I was trying not to chuckle at his analogy…after all, the conversations we have in our house are far from normal. As he began to get sleepy, he was mumbling as if he was talking to someone.

We were certain that our home was now clear of spirits, so perhaps they were following Jackson? Maybe he was attracting them; perhaps he was somehow a gateway to the other side? About a week after Jackson heard the lady's footsteps, I had put him to bed and was downstairs reading quietly when he came to the top of the stairs. When I asked him why he was up, he told me he heard footsteps in his room. I told him that I didn't hear anything, nor did the dog. I sent him back to bed and told him to leave his bedroom door open. About 10 minutes later, he was up again and told me he could still hear it. I said, "Tell the spirits in your room that you're tired and you want to go to sleep. Ask them to leave you alone and they will." He said he would, and lo and behold, that was the last I heard from him for the rest of the night, he slept like a baby.

Chapter 41

Make a Wish

During Jackson's stay at Holland-Bloorview, his doctor submitted an application on his behalf to The Make a Wish Foundation.

It was an ordinary day like any other; we had been home a few months by now. I went on the porch to check the mailbox. In there was a letter addressed to Jackson Kustra. When I opened it, I could not believe what I was reading. This letter brought tears to my eyes. Jackson had been granted a wish through The Make a Wish Foundation of Canada. In light of all that he had undergone, the foundation considered him a "specially deserving case".

He was really too young to even understand the meaning of such a special gift, but we tried to explain it to him in terms a 2½ yr old could understand.

We received a call from the foundation, saying that they would be sending representatives out from the

Southwestern Ontario Branch. These women wanted to come over and meet Jackson and discuss wish options with him.

As we sat around the kitchen table, we relayed his story to them and with tears in their eyes, they said if anyone ever deserved a wish it was Jackson. They let us know that he had until age 18 to use his wish and it could be almost anything he wanted as long as the wish was his. He had mentioned Disney Land on numerous occasions and so this is what we have told these wonderful volunteers that he desired for his special trip.

As I write this book, it has now been almost five years post stroke and we feel that Jackson is old enough (almost seven) to be able to enjoy his trip. He would be able to remember it, and have enough stamina to do it. We are scheduled to go this fall.

Many families go through difficulties, and once again, God has chosen to bless ours. Nightly around the dinner table and again at bedtime, I always reinforce to my children the need to thank God for all He has done for us. We can never take a minute of our lives for granted.

Chapter 42

Heaven Talk, between brothers

Timed Recording: 05/05/2015

Jackson being questioned by Lincoln about Heaven at bedtime:

Lincoln: "I need some information about what Heaven looks like".

Jack: "Heaven looks like lots of angels".

Lincoln: "What do angels look like? Do they have white wings?"

Jack: "Angels look like white and they're bright and they fly and they talk about HIM. They have noses and eyes and Heaven looks like it has a TV and it has a fun teeter-totter".

Lincoln: "Anything else?"

Jack: "No".

Lincoln: "Do you know what God looks like?"

Jack: "No".

Lincoln: "You didn't see HIM?"

Jack: "No".

Lincoln: "If you know what angels look like how come you don't know what God looks like?"

Jack: "I do but I just don't know what that man looks like, I just..."

Lincoln: "Do you know what His body looks like?"

Jack: "No, but I know what shape He is, but I just never seen Him".

Lincoln: "Not even when you were asleep? Not even in a dream?"

Jack: "No".

Lincoln: "Ok, thanks".

Jack: "You're welcome, now can you snuggle with me?"

Heaven Talk between Jackson and me
Timed Recording: 05/12/2015

I was asking Jackson about Heaven, this is our conversation:

Me: "Can you tell Mom what is your favorite thing about Heaven?"

Jack: "My favorite thing about Heaven is that you get to play on teeter-totters".

Me: "I love teeter-totters. Are there lots of them there?"

Jack: "No, just one".

Me: "I want you to describe it. What does it look like there?"

Jack: "So, either they burn your body or you get buried. And so, in Heaven you're in Heaven. Buildings all look brown like a marker and you can see Cisko (our departed dog) there and Jesus".

Me: "So how do people get around in Heaven, do they fly or do they walk?"

Jack: "They walk".

Me: "What kind of clothes do people wear there?"

Jack: "I don't know what kind of clothes they wear there. Do peoples' houses go to Heaven?"

Me: "No, I think God makes people a new house when they get there."

Chapter 43

The Chamber-HBOT Therapy

D uring my daily ride to the office, I would typically listen to 'WMUZ the Light', a Christian radio station based out of Detroit. During their commercial breaks, they would advertise the miraculous effects of Hyperbaric Oxygen Therapy. After hearing numerous claims of healing, I brought it up to my husband. At this point, we were 3 years post stroke in Jackson's recovery. Although he had made some nice gains, there were still some pretty significant deficits, despite physiotherapy three times a week.

He was still having issues with his balance and strength on his right side, as well as impaired walking and vision problems. The doctors were not giving us much hope for more improvement so we were looking into alternative treatments on our own. After doing considerable research, we both felt this was something that could potentially benefit Jackson.

We realized rather dejectedly that these treatments were offered only in Toronto (4hrs away) or in the US. Being a border city, this did not seem like that big of a sacrifice, until we discovered that Jackson would need to go daily for 40 consecutive days. They said we could omit weekends for a break. Each treatment was 1.5 hours in duration, so this would prove to be no small feat. Once again, we felt that we had run into a brick wall. How could we make this work with our work schedules and the boys' school schedule? Then once again, God did what only He can do; a clinic opened up right in our home city! Another miracle that I am so happy to share, this was going to be doable after all.

After touring the facility and speaking with the owner, we felt an immediate connection to this kind and gentle man. He and his wife owned two other facilities in the state of Michigan and had such a large client base in Windsor that they decided to open one up on this side of the border. He said that so many Canadians were seeking their services that it prompted them to consider opening up a Canadian branch. This was a tremendous and timely opportunity for Jackson!

It held a significant price tag though, $5,300 and not a cent of it was covered through our health care provider. Sometimes you have to step out on faith, no matter the cost. At this point, Jay and I would have given anything to give our son some semblance of a normal life again.

We decided to wait until school was out for the summer and start the treatment cycle then. This seemed to have the least impact on the home/work schedule. One of the benefits was that a parent could go in the chamber with the child. Some children tend to be scared or claustrophobic and this seemed to reduce the fear factor. This turned out to be a wonderful thing for my husband as he had been suffering with terrible back and knee pain at the time as a result of nearly 30 years in automotive manufacturing.

So began the daily morning ritual of Jay and Jackson entering the chamber together, pleasantly cool in their shorts, watching a movie and napping (for Dad) while Lincoln made himself comfortable on the couch watching movies.

The very first day of treatment was nothing short of miraculous. I came home from work to find Jackson running around the front yard with more energy than I had seen since we came home from hospital. He was laughing, running and playing as if this treatment had somehow awakened him. I honestly could not believe it. The next most curious thing was to find out how good my husband was feeling since he also spent an hour and a half in that clear oxygen filled chamber. He reported having very little pain in his back and he could not believe that he did not feel tired; after all, he was working the midnight shift at the time.

All I could think was if these results kept going like this, we would have our perfectly healthy son back in no time. I was so positive, so hopeful, I felt like this was the answer to all of my prayers. If this didn't heal him, nothing would. Therefore, the treatments went on day after day and amazingly, the results kept getting better and better, until about three weeks in. We started to notice that the results were not nearly as striking; he appeared to be at a plateau. However, we kept on with our course of treatment, ever hopeful that a miracle would take place. We both wanted the son we had before the stroke, the little boy whose life was just beginning...

Jackson was not made whole by this treatment, but we could never have lived with ourselves knowing that there was something out there for him and we didn't give it a shot. Perhaps my son is not meant to be perfectly whole, in the physical sense, but let me attest to his perfect wholeness in the spiritual sense. God sent him here on a mission, I am not sure what his purpose is, but judging by what I have already witnessed, he has amazing spiritual gifts to share with the world.

Chapter 44

Worn

When I think back on the last four years of my life, I realize that it is pitted with ups and downs. My husband and I have tried so hard to work through these trials, but I do feel my marriage has suffered a tremendous toll. We always prided ourselves on the fact that we made it through when the statistics say most do not.

We have always tried to be strong for the children, but ultimately they can see through the smoke screen. I do believe they realize the effect this has had on our home life. I have always leaned on God to help me through and He has carried me during the hardest times of my life.

When I thought I would lose Jackson to the stroke I cried out to my Father, I asked Him, begged Him, to let me keep my son. God answered my prayer and I am forever grateful.

However, I am so tired. It is a fatigue that is emotional, spiritual, and physical. Worn is the only way to describe the despair that tries to overtake me at times when I feel too weak to carry on. I have doubted that I am a good mother and wife; I feel that I have failed in many ways in my marriage. There are days that I feel like there is nothing left in my tank. Only those who have walked in my shoes can truly understand the depths of despair that I sometimes find myself in.

In moments like these, I reach for my bible, where I draw my strength and encouragement. God always sends me to the exact passage I need to give me the greatest comfort. Then, I go and tuck my children into bed and realize that these two beautiful angels were entrusted to my care for their earthly journey. I have a responsibility to pick myself up in faith and carry on for them. I must be the example God called me to be as their mother, to show them the way, to never give up and to always TRUST IN THE LORD.

Chapter 45

The Tall Stranger

He came for my son in the quiet of the night, leading him by the hand. This tall thin stranger that my son did not know, yet instinctively trusted. I am sure as Jackson looked down over his body, he felt scared or confused, and yet he went with him still.

As he entered this beautiful place, all he could feel was the peace surrounding him. He walked along a cobblestone path of the most stunning golden color; a narrow ravine followed the path. Hand in hand, he went with the tall, quiet stranger. They did not speak, at least not with their mouths and yet they shared their innermost thoughts. What I wouldn't give to know what was said between them. The only person I could presume this to be would be my Grandfather, a man I never had the chance to meet but always wished I had. He was my Father's father; a tall thin man with piercing blue eyes, much like my son's.

Never once did the doctors or nurses tell us that Jackson flat lined and yet my dear friend Veronica Green showed me this experience through a personal reading she did with Jackson when he was six years old. Not only had he encountered my father, but likely his great grandfather as well.

Jay and I knew that something extraordinary had happened to him when at the age of two and a half he began to describe Heaven in vivid detail. A place perhaps I once merely thought myth or conceptual, now seemed a very real place. According to Jackson, it is a place where all wishes come true. I now believe Heaven is a place where anything you wish or desire can be made manifest, according to the goodness of our Heavenly Father.

Chapter 46

Cherished Memories

I could not write this book and not share some of my fondest memories. They are in no particular order and they are as I remember them at the time.

It was a beautiful sunny day and we had been in the hospital for nine days. Auntie Jasna (my husband's sister) and her family had come to see Jackson. She brought him a bag full of books and toys, he was so happy! She also brought a big blanket and umbrella and the cousins played outside in the courtyard of the Ronald McDonald House. They laid in the sun, read books, and spent quality time together, just like old times. This was the happiest we had seen Jackson since the stroke happened. Here is the journal entry for that day:

Thursday Sept 22

Jack- I was soooo happy to see you today! Thanks for smiling at me! Today Daddy and I took you outside. It was a beautiful day to be outside. We played bubbles and balloons and laid on the picnic blanket together. We were so happy for you cause we knew how much you love the outdoors. Auntie Jasna got to give you your bath and dress you. Just because I love you buddy! I hope you liked the toys I brought (tambourine, piano, xylophone) all noise makers. See you soon….

Love Auntie Jasna

Xoxoxoxoxoxoxoxoxoxoxo

Another great memory was on a snowy winter's night. We had put Jackson to bed a bit early and took Lincoln sledding. On our excursions, we had stumbled upon the best spot for just this sort of outing. It started snowing late after dinner that night, light, fluffy snow, just the right kind for tobogganing.

This spot was near a walking trail and it had hills on all four sides. We pulled up around 9 pm and were surprised to find so many kids out at that late hour. Jay and I had also suited up with snow pants and boots; we were ready to do this. We were all desperate for a bit of fun at this point and we absolutely had the time of our lives. Lincoln could not seem to tire. He must have run up and down that hill dozens of times.

We left exhilarated, laughing and certainly cold and tired. We grabbed hot chocolate on our way back to the hospital and we knew that most of all Lincoln needed that. He needed just to be a five year old without any worries. It benefited us all greatly.

Another moment I will never forget is when my friend Jane showed up at the hospital in London. I had called her within a matter of days following Jack's diagnosis and she jumped on a plane from three provinces over to be at my side. She spent a full week with me at the hospital and was the pillar of strength I so desperately needed.

For the last five years, a few of us RMH families have chosen to celebrate our time together. We gather once a year to reminisce, to celebrate how far our children have come, and to fellowship together. I now consider these people my extended family.

Circumstances brought us together, and now nothing can keep us apart. Each year we eat, we laugh, and rejoice at how good God is. We serve an awesome God. Our children were all too young to understand what happened to them that brought us all together.

Five families from all different walks of life, come together through the most unimaginable heartache, yet we bring such joy to one another every year, year after year, and I do truly hope this tradition will continue for many more to come.

When people ask me about The Ronald McDonald House and what it means to me, I explain that it exemplifies the human essence of compassion. It brings families together; it creates bonds that for me will never be broken. I will NEVER forget what the House represented for me on that very dark day when my life bottomed out.

Chapter 47

These Days

S o much has happened since Jackson's stroke, most of it extremely positive, and definitely supernatural. Jackson began to describe Heaven as he experienced it at the tender young age of two and a half. This piqued my curiosity and lead to many lengthy and interesting discussions which I have shared with you.

Then, God took his experience and heightened it with images and scenes of angels, which I have also shared in these pages. Most recently, Jackson now has the ability to see color auras in people. If you ask him what color your angel is he can clearly tell you.

I have included the color auras so you can see the vastness of the color chart and their meanings.

Aura Colors and
Their Meaning

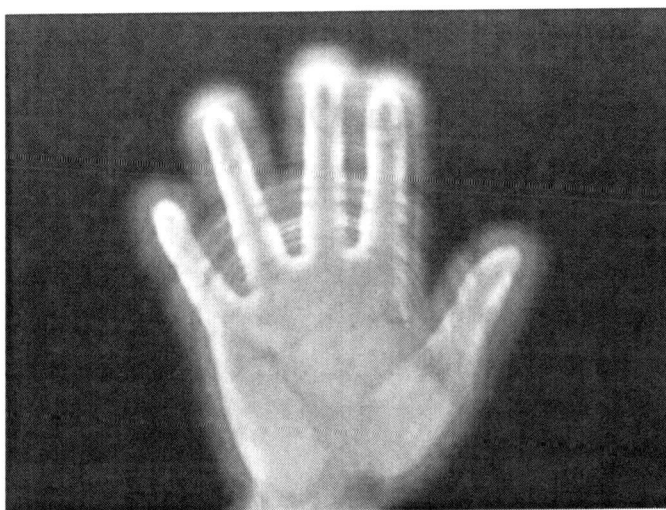

By Sally Painter
Paranormal Researcher and Seer

Auras can reveal information about your thoughts, feelings, dreams, and even others' wishes for you. Each color is not completely straightforward, however, and one must take into account the shade of a color in order to get an exact reading. Auras are given off by all living things because they emit energy with a special vibration and color. That color can be seen by gifted people and those trained in the healing arts, who can manipulate energy fields for effective healing.

About Aura Colors and Their Meanings

Auras come in all colors. It's rare to have only one color in <u>your aura</u>, although auras typically have one predominant color. Some can be a composite of rainbow colors.

Rainbow Auras

These auras are found in healers, especially those trained to work with the body's energy fields. These are typically seen as shards of colorful light, like a sunburst.

Yellow

<u>Yellow</u> has a specific physical correlation to the spleen and to the person's energy source, aka "chi."
- Brilliant yellow—You're spiritually inspired or experiencing a spiritual awakening. You have a playful spirit and will act on your thoughts.

- Dark yellow with tinges of brown–You're a student. You feel pressured to achieve your goals and score high on tests. You've lost your love of learning, and studying has become a tiresome chore.
- Lemon yellow–This represents a fear of loss. This may be the loss of a job, divorce, a lifestyle change, loss of health or fear of losing control over your destiny.
- Pale yellow–You've recently embarked on a spiritual journey, or you've discovered latent psychic abilities. There's a renewed sense of excitement and hope for the future.

Orange

Orange is associated with the reproductive organs and how a person's emotions are bound to that region of the body.

- Bright orange–This shade indicates good health, vibrancy and living life to its fullest. An overabundance of this hue could indicate you're trying to overcome an addiction or a desire.
- Orange-red–You wield great personal power and give off an air of confidence.
- Orange-yellow–You have a scientific mind and tend to be a bit of a perfectionist. You have a love for detailed work and mentally challenging projects.

Red

Red is one of the most powerful colors found in an aura. It can be a positive or a negative element. Red represents the blood. It's a vibration of action with the ability to either attract or repel.

- Dark red–You're centered and grounded to the earth, self-sufficient and able to survive any circumstance.
- Brilliant red–You are very passionate, sexual, full of energy and competitive.
- Clouded red–This represents a negative energy with deep-seated anger.
- Pink–You're a loving person. Pink indicates an artist, a sensual person who appreciates the finer things in life. If you've recently fallen in love, you'll have a significant amount of pink in your aura. Psychically gifted people also have pink auras.
- Dark pink–This color indicates deceit, dishonesty and an immature person.

Blue

This color represents the throat, specifically the thyroid. If your aura is blue, you're intuitive and you love helping people. You remain calm during a crisis. Others lean on you for support.

- Royal blue–This means you are a highly-developed spiritual intuitive or clairvoyant. You have a very generous and giving spirit, and you are always open to new possibilities.
- Dark blue, even cloudy–You don't trust the future and can't face the truth because of your desire to take control.
- Light blue–You're truthful and serene, and you excel in all fields of communication.

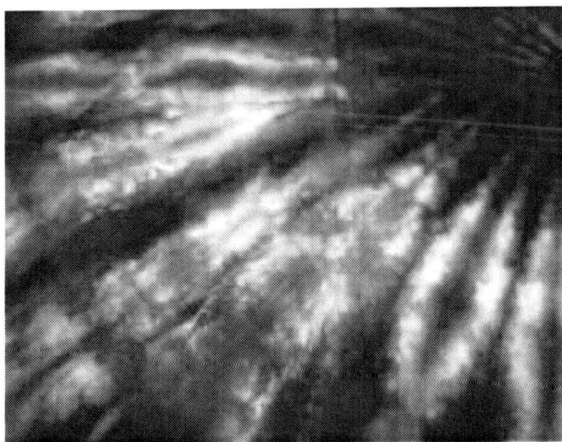

Green

Green is the color of the heart and of nature. This is usually found within the aura of healers, teachers and people who work for the public good.

- Forest green–You're a natural healer.
- Yellow-green–You're a communicator. You may be an actor, writer, musician or salesperson.
- Dark or cloudy green–You are very jealous person and full of resentment. You refuse to accept responsibility for your own actions.
- Turquoise–The ultra-aura color for a powerful healer. You help others discover their inner truths. Usually found in doctors, healers and counselors.

Purple hues

Purple is associated with the pituitary gland, pineal gland and the nervous system.

- Violet–You are a visionary of the highest level. You're someone who can daydream and change the world with spiritual love.
- Indigo–You get glimpses into other worlds and are a wise seeker.

Silver and Gold

Silver and gold auras are very positive and considered spiritual vibrations.

- Silver–This is the color of abundance. If shiny and bright, it indicates you have great physical and spiritual wealth.

- Gold–You have angels and other divine entities protecting you. You're being mentored and guided to reach beyond yourself.

Black

Black auras indicate you're holding on to negative feelings. Typically it indicates an unwilling and unforgiving spirit. This color can also indicate that disease is being held in certain regions of the body.

Other Dark Colors

Other dark colors can be indicators of blocked energy centers within the body.

- Gray–This color indicates blocked energy fields. You don't trust anyone or anything.
- Dark or murky brown–You're afraid to let go, and you're trying to hold on to your personal power or you're afraid to share yourself with others.

White

White typically indicates a newness and purity. It can be found in highly spiritual people who've transcended the physical and are preparing to ascend. Religious history claims white auras were seen surrounding angelic beings.

The fact that my son can now see auras leads me to wonder if he is destined to be a healer. I have felt the vibrational energy coming from his hands and if he puts his non-dominant hand on you, he will tell you he can feel the heat. This trait is found in Reiki healers.

Perhaps Jackson's story is not finished but merely just begun; perhaps the stroke was the catalyst for something so much bigger. Could it be that his gifts were lying in wait? The first two years of his life were merely preparing him for what was to come. God has definite plans for my son, a very special calling on his life and I feel blessed that He chose me to be his mother, to help nurture him along this divine journey.

I have come to accept this part of my life as my son's destiny. I can't change it, I can only look ahead. I have grown so much in my faith because of Jackson's illness. I would never undo it because I finally realize this was God's plan for our lives.

As for Jackson, he is a warrior. He has done battle with this illness and he has gained strength of mind, body and soul. His spiritual journey began when he was lifted up to heaven and shown things that most of us will only ever see and know upon death.

He walks daily with his spirit guides, and his angels surround him at night. I no longer worry for him; I know that the Divine protection he receives is so much greater than I could ever give him. I do not know where his journey will take him, but I do know that with Jesus at his right hand, he will excel at anything he chooses to do. He has received the blessing of a second chance at life. God would never extend that to him without expecting great things in return.

And so for now, life continues somewhat normally at the Kustra house. Jackson will soon be entering Grade two, and Lincoln, Grade five.

Jackson says he hates school, every day, and yet I hear from the teachers that he is constantly surrounded by many friends. I personally think it's because he would rather be home lying on the couch watching TV in his underwear while eating cheerios out of the box!

Jackson is definitely a homebody, he would rather be home than anywhere else. For the longest time we could not go anywhere for longer than an hour because he would be asking to leave. He is also very adamant that he is NEVER leaving home, or getting married. He insists that he will live with Mom and Dad forever.

He is a first class jokester, and is getting funnier by the day. He brings lots of humor to our household and sometimes we need a good laugh or we would just cry.

He is moody and temperamental, yet kind and sensitive all at once. Lately he is into art and enjoys drawing. All of his pictures have rainbows and our family in them. He brought home an award from school 'The Amazing Artist Award'. He proudly displays all his works of art on my refrigerator, so many in fact that you cannot tell what color my fridge is! He loves animals and being outdoors. Frisbee is his new passion and learning to swim.

Jackson is very deep and complex and sometimes it's hard to understand just what he's thinking. Jay and I always say he's an adult in a child's body. The way he analyzes a situation and then comes up with a solution, makes you feel like you are talking to an adult rather than a six-year-old.

Health wise he is doing as well as can be expected, no significant improvements at this stage. He is carrying around a bit too much weight, but food is his best friend. We are trying to teach him healthy eating habits but I am afraid that he may be eating his feelings. With daily bike rides and constant swimming, I am hopeful that he will shed some weight, which will in turn help to improve his mobility. A neurologist is no longer following him; only if there appears to be any changes do we need to follow up. He is going to require eye surgery this fall to correct damage to the muscles of the eyes caused by the stroke. We are hopeful that the doctors can correct this easily enough and his vision will be ok in the end. He will continue to wear a special brace on his right leg for greater stability while walking and standing.

Overall, I think Jackson is well adjusted and happy. He does have some days that he is down and emotional. He asks me why God made him have a disability. I tell him I believe he was specially chosen by God because he has very important work to do. Perhaps he is meant to teach us all some very valuable lessons; namely empathy and compassion.

Then there is Lincoln, our very mature ten-year-old. He is well liked by everyone and is compassionate, gentle, kind and sincere. His teachers sing his praises; they all adore him.

He has many friends and seems to adjust easily to any situation. He loves sports and is good at most of them. This year he has taken an interest in baseball, to Grandpa's delight! He joined the Riverside Baseball Association's house league and was then picked up by the travel team whose coaches saw the raw talent that he possesses. Lincoln placed third in two different events at his very first track and field meet. I do believe he is a natural athlete, which he sure did not inherit from me.

Lincoln loves attending church on Sundays and has expressed his desire to be baptized, which we are planning for this fall. My first-born is a bit more serious than most, a result I suspect from witnessing his brother's ordeal. I do realize that he gets frustrated sometimes, not living with a 'normal brother'. Most ten year olds do not have to wipe bums or help their brother put his shoes on. I love my son dearly for the amazing person he is, the loving heart he has and the compassion he displays so freely. I do pray that he works hard and strives to get everything he is deserving of in this life and even more in the next.

Jay and I are weary and emotional at times, but God has demonstrated miracles through our son, enough to sustain us through the hard times and reassure us of better days ahead. It has certainly not been an easy road, but one that took great courage on all of our parts. Ultimately, we are a family, and families figure things out. We tough it out when times are hard, we love deeply, and we respect the fact that this has all affected us differently. We just love each other, as we should all be doing every day of our lives. In this house, we choose 'happy'.

Epilogue

The Star Fairy came for Jackson's star. She placed it in the sky of the Castle of Miracles. This would ensure that Jackson would always have a special place at Give Kids The World Village. This star represents Jackson as one of over 100,000 children to have come through The Village. This unique place is like no other I have ever experienced. It is a place where parents and children alike can share in their struggles, understand each other's pain, but most importantly, get away from it all.

This trip truly was the most amazing experience of our lives. Jackson was blessed with this trip by Make a Wish Foundation, Southwestern ON. They sent our family on a week-long trip of a lifetime, at least to our seven year old. Epcot, Universal Studios, The Magic Kingdom all held fun and fascination, however what my kids loved most, 'family time'.

Give Kids The World Resort is only for Wish Children and their families. It was an enchanted Candy Land where you could eat ice cream for breakfast, take a train ride through the park, ride the carousel, or soar high on the butterfly ride. A place where you could watch movies in your very own movie theatre and eat all the popcorn you wanted.

This magical place had goofy golf and fishing, horseback riding, and two pools with a splash pad. Why would any child want to leave? No wonder Jackson woke up crying on the seventh day. We were all a bit emotional to be leaving this paradise.

I am sure that for the first time in Jackson's life, he felt like he completely fit in here. This place was acceptance, it was empathy, it was extreme compassion. 1700 volunteers give of their time and talents each day to ensure that the village runs smoothly for every family that walks through their door.

Jackson will have a permanent marker in front of the carousel. We purchased a paving stone in his honour to commemorate our stay at Give Kids The World Village. His 'Avenue of Angels Paver' is one of hundreds that make up the cobblestone walkways known as 'The Walkway of Love' that run throughout The Village. We look forward to visiting next year and seeing his memory permanently etched into this beautiful place. We are eager to spend the day volunteering and giving back, by blessing others.

My very mature ten year has decided that he is ready to take the step of baptism. We celebrated this event during Sunday service over Thanksgiving weekend. I could not think of anything I would be more thankful for than that. He is peacefully content in his decision and proudly wears his 'I Have Decided' t-shirt to school where he openly talks to his peers about Jesus.

I could not be more proud of the young man he's becoming. Lincoln is once again playing floor hockey to whittle away the winter months until baseball season returns. He is enthralled with Supernatural and Prison Break, guaranteed you will find him in his room glued to his tablet!

Jackson currently takes Spanish lessons on Saturday mornings and tells me that he is a "muchacho bueno" or good boy in English! He loves it and is the star of the class. Legos are still his passion and every day the creations get more elaborate. The imagination on this child never ceases to amaze me.

As for Jay and I, we are still living a crazy hectic life. We are like ships passing in the night, hi and bye is all we seem to say to each other. My nine to five job and his midnight shift are not kind to our relationship. This is why we enjoyed our vacation so much; we actually had a chance to reconnect. We both understand the value this adds to our marriage and are trying to carve out more time for us.

Overall, we are happily adjusted and live in appreciation each day. We try not to look too far ahead, for tomorrow is not promised.

It is my hope that our story touches you in some way, that it draws you close to The Father, and offers you hope of the beautiful eternity that awaits each one of us.

Love and Blessings,
Serena

Jackson and family,
Thank you so much for
the BEAUTIFUL gift! I will
hang it proudly in my
new classroom. It has been
an absolute pleasure to
work with Jackson this year,
he is one of the most amazing
kids I've ever encountered!
I hope your family has a
wonderful summer together

♡ miss Maxim

CPSIA information can be obtained
at www.ICGtesting.com
Printed in the USA
LVOW11s1136020517

532887LV00001B/2/P